THE CROSS IN AGONY AND ECSTASY

THE CROSS IN AGONY AND ECSTASY

Lenten Sermons

Herbert F. Lindemann and George F. Lobien

Publishing House
St. Louis   London

Concordia Publishing House, St. Louis, Missouri
Concordia Publishing House Ltd., London, E. C. 1
Copyright © 1973 Concordia Publishing House
Library of Congress Catalog Card No. 72-89625
ISBN 0-570-06383-3

MANUFACTURED IN THE UNITED STATES OF AMERICA

Contents

Mysteries
By Herbert F. Lindemann

Crossroads
By George F. Lobien

Mysteries

By Herbert F. Lindemann

Preface

Materialistic — mechanistic — scientific — secularistic: these are some of the adjectives used to describe our civilization. None of them leaves room for much awe, wonder, and belief in the miraculous. Yet, however obscured and undefined, there is in man an insatiable hunger for something beyond the things that are seen, something which can give him the peace, love, and joy which no human achievement seems able to convey. St. Augustine pointed to the satisfaction of this desire when he said, "Thou hast made us for Thyself, and our souls are restless until they find rest in Thee."

These sermons have been written in the hope of facilitating man's discovery of the mysterious yet revealed God, and in this experience to find the fulfillment of his deepest longings. It won't be perfect, of course; nothing in this world ever is. The best we can hope for is some intimation of the glory which is to come. Sometimes, however, this intimation becomes very strong; some religious experience takes place. Perhaps the sermons on the mysterious God will pave the way for such an experience. In any event, they may well point to its possibility. For the mysterious God yearns to be discovered.

HERBERT LINDEMANN

This Mysterious World

John 8:59: "Jesus was not to be seen." (NEB)

Bruce Marshall has written an altogether delightful story called *Father Malachy's Miracle*. Father Malachy is one of those rare Christian souls who are always living in a world where God makes the impossible come to pass. He emerges from a long seclusion in a monastery to accept an assignment in a parish church and is hardly established in his new position when he meets a neighboring minister of another denomination who disbelieves all miracles, those of our Lord's incarnation and resurrection included. Amazed and angered by this man's unbelief, Father Malachy guarantees to perform a miracle that very night. And at the agreed hour the miracle takes place.

It has to do with a dance hall across the street from the church which is corrupting the youth of the neighborhood. Shortly before the zero hour the priest has his colleagues lay out vestments for a service of thanksgiving and light all the candles in the sanctuary. Then they proceed to the street before the dance hall, where, after a moment of prayer, Father Malachy, in the name of the blessed Trinity, commands the building to be removed to an island in the sea. Promptly the structure rises from its foundation and flies through the air to the designated spot. The priests then return to the church and don their vestments, Father Flaherty goes to the organ loft and pulls out all the stops, and they sing a mighty Te Deum.

11

Now comes the real point of the story. Nobody next day will believe that a miracle has occurred. The hole in the ground where the dance hall used to be is thoroughly inspected, and various parties row out to the new site on the island; but everyone agrees that there must be some good, rational explanation for it. Especially the learned men are adept at explaining the miracle away. And the story ends when Father Malachy, greatly discouraged, moves the dance hall back to its original place.

Marshall is saying something that is all too true: most men nowadays refuse to believe in the miracles that happen constantly, to say nothing of those that are part of recorded history. Even Christian people do not have the same sense of the mysterious that characterized the church of former generations. If we run into something that seems mysterious, we are quite sure that, once we have investigated and analyzed and learned to understand, it will appear mysterious no longer. To proceed in any other way strikes us as being unenlightened, prescientific, superstitious.

Sometimes, indeed, we become a bit wistful about this and look back enviously to the time when the knowledge of mankind was a good deal less than it is now. Life was much simpler then, and the faith by which men lived seemed sure and satisfactory. There were tight little answers to all questions which none but the damned ever thought of challenging. Now all that is gone, and life is chaotic, and men are of the opinion that, although God may have seemed marvelous to a less tutored generation, He cannot mean much to us, who see through everything.

Most men, however, in spite of all the insecurities of our age, are glad they are alive today. There are incalculable advantages to being alive in the last third of the twentieth century. It's a thrilling experience, somewhat breathtaking and confusing but for the most part immensely fascinating. The explosion of knowledge, the discoveries and inventions of science are such that preoccupation with all of it has become our most prominent characteristic. We are astounded by it and delighted with it, and there are very few of us who would willingly give it all up and embrace a primitive kind of life again. How would we get along without electricity, running water, and speeding vehicles? What would we do with our time if we didn't have television? How ghastly it would be if we had no defense against the plague, diphtheria, polio! It's unthinkable!

The Christian faith does not require this of us. It does not even require us to hold on with one hand to all the achievements of modern times, and with the other to reach back desperately to the ages of faith. To look wistfully to the past is to miss seeing the Christ who strides on ahead. This was the sin of Lot's wife. To do this is to imply that, though God may have done great things in former days, He has now more or less retired from active duty. Christ is not only a historical figure; He is a living person. He has not exhausted His power by performing the miracles that are recorded in the Bible. In fact He said, "Greater things than these shall you do." Can we get it into our heads that He said this to the church for all time? Our task is to believe in the God "in whom we live and move and have our being," the God who is the same wonderful, wonder-working God whom we encounter on the pages of the Bible. His mysteries are with us still.

The purpose of these sermons is to make us a bit more aware of these mysteries of God. More: it is to propose the thesis that the mysteries have become much more mysteries precisely because of our expanding knowledge. If the universe was wonderful to our ancestors, it is far more wonderful to us, who peer through microscopes and telescopes and conduct innumerable experiments in countless laboratories. Every day we come upon some new wonder as the secrets of nature are progressively exposed. The marvels which God has put into His world surpass in overwhelming quantity the most lively imagination of ancient times. It's important to keep on being conscious of this.

The more prominent of these mysteries we shall be talking about in subsequent sermons. For the moment let us agree on their reality, that the mysteries of God are indeed mysteries. No one comes at them who does not believe them to be and is furthermore willing to be led and guided by various clues to their discovery. These things are not approached in the same way we undertake the study of scientific truth, for they belong in a different category from the axioms of algebra or the propositions of geometry. We do not master these mysteries at all; they master us. This means that we must deal with them in humility and reverence, with a sense of wonder, or they will forever elude us.

There are tragic words at the end of the eighth chapter of John, the chapter that records a furious verbal boxing match between our Lord and the Pharisees. The words are: "Jesus was not to be seen." You feel the sheer pathos of the tragedy when you read this; it's like the shutting of a door in their faces, the tolling of the bell over their dead souls. The worst of it was that it was so unnecessary. There He was, right in front of them, and they did not recognize Him. And this was because they weren't looking for Him in the right place. They kept thinking about their glory-filled past. "We are Abraham's descendants; we have never been in slavery to any man." "Abraham is our father." So they kept on looking back to the things that were gone, that used to be, brushed aside the eternal present, and took up stones to throw at Him.

That they did so is evidence that they were moving in a different world from His. Theirs was a world of suspicions, prejudices, and hates that were rooted in history, and as long as they were entangled in all that, they were in no condition to become worshipers of the Savior. You've got to be free of all that if you're going to be "lost in wonder, love, and praise." You must recognize that the place you're standing on is holy ground. You must stop running for awhile; you must kneel down and look up. You must spend some time in contemplation; as Brother Lawrence did, you must "practice the presence of God."

To modern minds this seems like a waste of time. It is much more important to get on with the job, to do something, to be active. We shall therefore have to make up our minds at the outset whether God's mysteries are realities or not. If they are, there can be no higher good, no greater blessing than to become immersed in them. This is about the same as saying that the basic choice is between faith and atheism. For if we believe in God, we are moved inexorably to follow through from that fundamental assumption. "Anyone who comes to God must believe that He exists and that He rewards those who search for Him" (Heb. 11:6). He does indeed. And searching for Him means to be like children: guileless, trusting, accepting, ready for joy. "This is our Father's world, and it is beautiful and wonderful."

The Mystery of the Trinity

A mystery, by definition, is something hidden, yet capable of being known. Its secret may be discovered, but only by one who penetrates beneath the surface of things. In the New Testament the word "mystery" never means sheer mystery. It always means a divine secret which it has pleased God to reveal to men, a secret so mysterious that human beings could never even begin to discover it by themselves. But God, says the New Testament, has taken the initiative and disclosed the secret. The secret has to do with the nature of God Himself. It is summed up in the Christian doctrine concerning the Holy Trinity.

What is this doctrine? We turn instinctively for an answer to the catechism or the Athanasian Creed, and in doing so we are partly right and partly wrong. We are right because what we have called "sheer mystery" is not enough; that is, every genuine mystery must not only have a mysterious atmosphere but also, and more importantly, a kernel of reality. The reality in this case is the three-personal God, and the dogmaticians are quite right in putting this into words as they may. But if we think that reading these theological statements and agreeing with them puts us into contact with the living God, we are tragically wrong.

We shall do well to be on our guard against this. It is a common assumption — although anyone who falls into the

16

trap invariably denies it — that Christianity is all neatly spelled out for us in the catechism and that, when one has completed a course of preconfirmation instruction, one knows all there is to know about God. The point of the instruction, however, is — or ought to be — that God is not so much to be understood as He is to be worshiped. He is not defined in answer to the question: What is God? He is rather pointed to as One who is infinitely wonderful, beautiful, glorious, powerful, just, and loving. These are not qualities to be comprehended with the mind; they move us to adoration of the soul.

This is why the attempt to set down the teachings of Christianity in perfectly exact language, in such a way that there will be no possible error of definition, is hopeless and useless. God cannot be confined in human words. Always there will remain something elusive, something that defies all description. This is why St. Paul concludes one of his discussions of a doctrine with the exclamation that forms the major part of the Epistle for Trinity Sunday: "O depth of wealth, wisdom, and knowledge in God! How unsearchable His judgments, how untraceable His ways!"

This is of vital importance for the whole work of Christian education. No sane Christian would deny that education lies close to the heart of the church's mission; the last thing our Lord said to His disciples before He ascended into heaven was that they should go and teach. In fulfillment of this command we spend a tremendous amount of time, energy, and money to acquaint people with the truths of the faith. There are full-time and part-time schools on every educational level, Bible classes, institutes, and workshops galore.

But even as we go about this work, we need to be aware

that, in dealing with the things of God, there is a limit to what may be understood. It is as the eighteenth-century mystic Gerhard Tersteegen said: "A God understood, a God comprehended, is no God." This is why, in our times, so much is being written and done in the art of worship. Thousands of Christians, as they have learned to practice this art, have been exhilarated by the experience. For the kind of God we need is the real God, and He is One who transcends our words and stretches our thoughts, so that we have to leave the schoolroom behind and use poetry and music, symbols and sacraments and ceremonies and all the solemn and mysterious decorum of Christian worship. In doing so we but reflect the attitudes of the Biblical writers, who time after time cease being teachers and break out into hymns of praise and adoration. "Great beyond all question," says St. Paul, "is the mystery of our religion."

This does not mean that our religion is irrelevant to our daily lives. On the contrary, it is as pertinent as anything can be. For the mystery is the mystery of love, since the essence of it is God, and He, as St. John says, "is Love." This Triune God is something quite different from a dogmatic statement that tells us we must "neither confound the Persons nor divide the Substance." He becomes alive in our souls only when we reflect that the Father, back in an unimaginable eternity, set His love upon us and determined to bring us to Himself; that the Son, in the fullness of time, redeemed us to God by His blood; and that the Holy Spirit, when we finally appeared on the stage of history, has worked ceaselessly — even after we came to believe the Gospel — to bring its truth to bear on our somewhat unresponsive souls.

The result is that every Christian is confronted with

the absolutely staggering truth that the three Persons of the Godhead have exerted Themselves to bring about his redemption, that, indeed, this seems to be Their chief concern, toward the achievement of which They devote Themselves with all of Their powerful love. They never interfere with a man's freedom, but They do call, invite, urge, exhort, proclaim, testify, witness — whatever verb may be used to describe the working of divine grace.

When one considers for whom all this was done and is being done, that the object of God's love is sinful men, with all the dreadful associations of that word "sinful," then the mystery of this love becomes utterly incomprehensible. As St. Paul says, one could understand it if Christ had died for righteous men, but His laying down His life for sinners is just too much for us to grasp. Yet the fact of it is there, a fact not to be comprehended but to be accepted as the basis for adoration.

This is why the liturgy — which is another word for corporate worship — is so full of references to the Holy Trinity. The service begins in the name of the Father, Son, and Holy Spirit. The absolution is pronounced in the same name. The faithful give glory to the Triune God after the psalm of the Introit. There is a reference to the three Persons in the threefold petition of the Kyrie. The Gloria in Excelsis ends with an ascription of praise: "You alone are the Most High, Jesus Christ, with the Holy Spirit, in the glory of God the Father." The termination of the collect is trinitarian. The Creed, of course, has its three articles. The Sanctus with its threefold "holy" hints at the same thing; so does the Agnus Dei. The Nunc Dimittis has the Gloria Patri attached to it, and the Benediction is tripartite. Thus at every step of the way we express our faith in the one God who is three Persons. Evidently the church thinks this is very important.

The question is how important we as individuals think it to be. It is one thing to brush it aside as one of those pieces of theological hairsplitting that cannot possibly have any significance for people in this scientific age; it is quite another to appreciate its relevance to our need. Actually the heart of the doctrine is anything but abstract; the historical facts of the Gospel are quite concrete.

And this is what helps us in our weakness. When we feel that God is remote, when we don't know how to conceive of Him, when we cry with the ancient prophet, "Oh, that Thou wouldst rend the heavens and come down" (Is. 64:1), then the Christian Gospel assures us that this is exactly what He has done in Jesus Christ. It was done in a town called Bethlehem, at a time when Caesar Augustus ruled the Roman Empire. And if this still seems to leave God somewhat remote to our twentieth-century living, we may go to our parish church and hear Christ's Word sounding in our ears and receive His body and blood at the rendezvous which He has appointed. While we are there, we shall certainly say the Gloria Patri at least once. Perhaps it would be a good idea, as we do so, to emphasize the little words "is now."

For God has done all that could be done to make Himself accessible. He remains behind a veil, but it is veritably He who is there. His voice is gone out into all the earth. He besets us behind and before; we cannot flee from His Spirit or escape from His presence. Ceaselessly He presses in on every one of us with His inexorable love. He claims us, He wants to befriend us and make us like Himself. It's a thing to be received with adoration and praise.

"Great is the mystery of our religion!" "Glory to the Father and to the Son and to the Holy Spirit; as in the beginning, so now and forever. Amen."

Mysteries of God

1 Corinthians 4:1: ". . . the mysteries of God."

The Jews, writes St. Paul to the Corinthians, were always asking for a sign, for some spectacular phenomenon that would stamp the word spoken to them as authentic and the speaker of it as one truly sent from God. But the Jews are not the only ones who look for a sign. We too would appreciate some audible or visible approval from God Himself of this parish or of our denomination, so that all the world would know that the Word uttered here is verily His Word and that our work is His work. Such a testimonial would be an invaluable advertisement. It would put an end once and for all to the notion that what we say here week after week is nothing more than our own ideas about what is true and how men should live. It would also help a great deal to bring order into the chaos of denominationalism; it would let the world know definitely that we Lutherans are right! So, like the Jews, we too, in our pride and arrogance, hanker after a sign.

But there is no such sign forthcoming. Our Lord told the Jews that no sign would be given them except His own death and resurrection. He says the same thing to us. The work of the church is not accompanied by voices from heaven or all manner of miracles on earth. Miracles do indeed occur, but they are rare. For the most part the life of the church goes on without anything startling happening, and the outsider is therefore apt to conclude that nothing whatever is taking place, that the whole business is nothing but meaningless mumbo-jumbo which an enlightened modern may well do without. This is a difficulty which the church has always had to face. The Holy Spirit does His work under cover, as it were: invisibly, intangibly, mysteriously. It is to this process that we now address ourselves: to the here-and-now advent of God into the hearts of men, the present coming of our Lord to which St. Paul refers when he says: "Let a man so account of us as of the ministers of Christ and stewards of the mysteries of God." Our subject then is these "Mysteries of God."

The difficulty with these mysteries, as St. Paul states it in another place, is that "we have this treasure in earthen vessels." Our problem then is to stop looking at the outside of the vessels and behold the treasure that's inside. Or as Luther expressed it, we need to pull the sword from the scabbard. Somehow we must get behind the appearance of things to see them as they really are. Our Lord often taught in parables, and some got the point of them and some did not. "If you have ears, then hear," said Jesus. There were those that heard but did not hear, just as they saw Him but did not recognize Him. The secrets of God's kingdom are not self-evident facts to be memorized but mysterious truths to be believed. These hidden things are revealed only to the believing soul.

They are revealed, the Scriptures say, in the Word. Now this is in itself a mysterious process. For when we talk about the Word, we do not mean just the imparting of information. This Word is peculiar to God, just as your words are peculiar to you and mine to me. "Your accent gives you away," as someone said to Peter in Caiphas' courtyard. Your words reveal what you are. For example, if you say, "I've been waitin' on you," everyone knows you're from Indiana. But there is more to it than that.

Words are expressive of the very personality of the speaker. This can be seen most clearly in poets. When you hear the lines, "I wandered lonely as a cloud that floats on high o'er vales and hills," you will say immediately, if you had a good course in English literature, "That's Wordsworth!" "The arrows of outrageous fortune" will make you exclaim, "That's Shakespeare!" "If I should die, think only this of me, that there's some corner of a foreign field that is forever England"—Rupert Brooke. "I must go down to the seas again, to the lonely sea and the sky"—John Masefield.

By saying these names you mean a little something more than that so-and-so wrote the lines attributed to him; you mean that the words carry with them some of the personality of the author. This was how he thought, this was how he felt, this is typically he. The same is true of music, painting, sculpture, architecture, indeed of anything at all that is typical of the person who produced it. Any expression of personality bears the trademark of the person; it is peculiar to him; it could have been expressed by no one else in exactly the same way.

Well, then, when you hear the words "Blessed are the merciful" or "All power is given unto Me" or "Go and do thou likewise," you say at once that these are the words of Jesus Christ. And here again you don't mean merely that He said them but that they conveyed and still do convey something of His personality, His mind and heart, Himself. This is He; and we rightly say that when such words are uttered, He is really present, speaking to us yet again, trying to get us to know Him and enter into fellowship with Him.

24

This is why we sing "Glory to You, O Lord" before the Gospel, and "Praise to You, O Christ" after it. We are not addressing these sentiments to an absentee Lord or to a Christ who is merely a personage in the history of mankind but to One who is verily in the midst of us as He promised to be. The words that we hear could not possibly be spoken by anyone else.

Yet they are uttered by men like me, and this creates the aforementioned difficulty: that those who hear the words must somehow perceive them to be not the words of some run-of-the-mill preacher but of Christ Himself. The preacher or the sermon or the Bible itself—these are the earthen vessels. The vessels are expendable, but the treasure contained in them is of infinite and eternal value. This is the "hidden wisdom" that St. Paul talks about. To the faithless man, he says, the Gospel is foolishness, but to the believing soul it is the power of God. It is only by faith that we come at the mystery.

Try then to realize, when you come to church, that it is God who is addressing you, confronting you. He does this through human beings who don't represent Him as they should, and in words which at best do not convey the full force of what He wants to say. But how else should God convey His meaning? He can best get through to us on our own level; this is the whole significance of the Incarnation. When Jesus taught the people, there were some vocal chords at work in the throat of a man, facial expressions that could be noted, and gestures of hands and arms. The risk He took was that men should see and hear no more than a human being like themselves.

God is still taking that risk. In countless sermons, lectures, and books men use myriads of words—and sometimes we preachers use far too many of them. But God's great purpose is that the men who hear and read these words will hear the Word of God, will catch at least some echo of the music of eternity sounding through the cacophony of time. And when, as one of our Introits puts it, the Lord causes His glorious voice to be heard, then do we have gladness of heart. At least some of us do. There are others who are bored, sleepy, resentful, hostile, critical, and unbelieving. For them the same thing is happening as happened long ago when the Jews looked at our Lord and sniffed, "Is not this Joseph's son? What good thing can come out of Nazareth?" They were not able, you see, to penetrate to the hidden truth of Christ's deity; and later on the preaching of Christ crucified was to them a stumbling block and to the Greeks foolishness.

So today: As Jesus could be met without being recognized, the Bible can be read and preaching can be heard without the Word of God being perceived. Indeed, printed and spoken words can become the prison and grave of vital truth, so that, as our Lord said of the Jews, "They look without seeing and listen without hearing or understanding." It were better for such people if they never came into contact with the Word of God at all. For this is not a thing to be played with. He who hears the Word must not do so "unadvisedly or lightly but reverently, discreetly, and in the fear of God."

"He who comes near Me comes near fire," runs an apocryphal saying of our Lord. This is something that needs to be remembered by church members who from childhood on have heard and used the living Word until it has become commonplace to them. "How much torpidity of soul, how much total iciness and dryness of spiritual life can issue from the fact that men, in year-long habit, in hasty copious words, are occupied in spiritual babbling about Christ, without knowing and considering Him to be what He is, the mystery of God that has been revealed, in whom God visits His children for their salvation. This mystery is a dangerous reality. 'He who comes near Me comes near fire.'"

But a fire need not burn; it can warm and it can purify. Sometimes we have that experience when the Holy Spirit, speaking through some preacher, will really get through to us, so that we go home from church feeling cleansed and inspired. Various factors go into such an experience. One is our own receptivity at the moment. Another is the materials of the service: hymns, lessons, prayers, music, etc. A third, and perhaps the most important, is the manner in which the sermon is preached. It is just not true to say that it makes no difference how a preacher preaches, that it is the Word of God just the same. It does make a difference. In some men and in some sermons there is more of the divine than in others; and this makes things easier for the listeners.

But in all men and in all sermons — assuming that they are orthodox — there is some admixture of these two elements, for this is God's way of doing things. "It hath pleased Him by the foolishness of preaching to save them. that believe." The problem for the listener — and this is a thing of considerable difficulty — is to get past the preacher to the Christ who stands behind him and should be in him, to crack the earthen vessel and get at the treasure. For the purpose of all preaching is that people may say after it is over, not: "What a wonderful sermon that was," but: "What a great God that is!" As Luther said in his Preface to the

Old Testament, "Here wilt thou find the swaddling-clothes and crib in which Christ lies, to which the angel guided the shepherds. Poor and mean are the swaddling-clothes, but precious is the treasure that lies therein—Christ!"

This is always the heart and center of everything. It is necessary whenever we undertake to use the Word and sacraments and prepare to receive them, that we believe and remember that the Savior Himself lies concealed behind these audible and visible forms. If then we listen attentively and open our eyes to all that can be seen, it may be that we shall become aware that "Jesus of Nazareth is passing by."

The Mystery of the Incarnation

**1 Timothy 3:16: "He . . . was manifested in the body."
(NEB)**

We have already begun to see, in this series of sermons, that again and again in his writings St. Paul speaks of
the mystery of God. The sentence just before our text is
one instance of this. He says: "Great beyond all question
is the mystery of our religion." What specifically does he
refer to? He goes on to tell us in words that sound as if
they may have been used as an act of worship in the
churches of his day; they have a liturgical atmosphere about
them. Today we shall look at only the first phase; next
time we'll discuss the others. It is our blessed Lord, of
course, who is spoken of throughout.

"He . . . was manifested in the body." This is the basic
mystery, what C. S. Lewis calls the "Grand Miracle." This
is the impossible thing come to pass, that

>"Disguised in our poor flesh and blood
>Is now the everlasting Good."

Therefore Chesterton describes the wise men as "following the way of the wandering star, to the things that cannot
be and that are." So too our Lord said to His disciples:
"Many prophets and kings wished to see what you now see,
yet never saw it." For the Incarnation was something which
in former ages was a secret, passed on at first by word of
mouth and later by the chosen people, concerning a won-

29

derful deed which God had promised to do one day, a deed by which a new age would be introduced into the world.

Not everyone by any means knew about this, and among those who did know there was naturally a good deal of wondering as to what the promised Deliverer would be like and how He would carry out His mission. There were the inspired prophecies, of course, and there was the symbolism of the temple ritual; but these were at best only hints of what was to come. St. Paul calls them "shadows," and the epistle to the Hebrews refers to them as types and figures. The reality, the fulfillment, was not seen until the advent of our Lord. Then the invisible God was manifested, so that St. John shouts: "We have seen it with our own eyes; we looked upon it and felt it with our own hands!" This is the surpassingly wonderful event which is the heart of history and the basis for all our adoration.

Thus in one sense the mystery is no longer a mystery; God has made Himself known in Jesus Christ. Now our knowledge of God is all focused through this one Person. In these New Testament times we have to do not with something anonymous and vague, a "First Cause or Primal Reason in which all our thoughts sink and vanish, the rayless depths of which swallow up all shapes and concepts. But the divine mystery is present amongst us as a figure that we can see, as a bodily form, as the other Adam whom God has raised up by His creative Spirit and shaped out of earthly matter. . . . Christ is not simply one sublime figure in the Valhalla of human greatness, but in the historical manifestation of Jesus Christ God Himself actually enters into the ranks of mankind, so that Christ's life is really God's life; His love, God's love; His power is really God's power; His fight is God's fight, His victory is God's."

30

"There is no salvation in anyone else at all," says St. Peter. Rudolph Staehlin pinpoints it this way: "Not anywhere in all the wide world, not in any one among the innumerable forms of manifestations of the Godhead, but in this concrete form dwells the whole fullness of the Godhead. . . . In this hour of history, at this place of the world, within this despised and unworthy nation, in this definite and unrepeatable life of man, something has taken place which cannot be paralleled by all other events of the world's history." "No one has ever seen God; but God's only Son, He who is nearest to the Father's heart, He has made Him known."

However, we must not suppose that this epiphany now makes all things intelligible, so that we now understand all mysteries and have all knowledge. For the Incarnation is in itself a most tremendous mystery. It is an ancient Christian custom to kneel or to bow deeply at the words of the Nicene Creed: "and was incarnate by the Holy Ghost of the Virgin Mary and was made man." The church acknowledges thereby that here "God has visited His people." And this acknowledgement is made with deepest reverence.

"A great and mighty wonder" it is that the divine should become human, the infinite finite, the immortal mortal, the spiritual physical. It is indeed so astounding a fact that to this day many people cannot bring themselves to believe it. Nineteen hundred years ago Jesus was crucified precisely because He claimed to be the Christ, the Son of the Blessed; because He said: "Before Abraham was born, I am"; because He told the Jews they would see Him in glory, coming on the clouds of heaven. This to them was an incredible idea, and so it is today.

On the face of it it seems absurd that the helpless Child

of Mary, the humble Man of Nazareth, the crucified Victim of Calvary should be the Same by whom all things were made. This is the offense of the cross, because of which God comes to His own and His own receive Him not. Here is the risk that God took in humbling Himself, a risk that proves too much for many a man. This is why, no doubt, St. Paul speaks of the Gospel as a mystery. There is a secret here, something hidden and strange. Only those who permit themselves to be shown, who surrender themselves trustingly to the guidance of the Spirit, only they discover the truth that is waiting to be revealed.

So we come at this paradox, that the mystery of our religion is revealed and concealed at the same time. Christ is "manifested in the body," but His very body is a covering for the majesty of God. For His part God intends that His becoming man should be the means of making Himself known, but for unbelieving man the Incarnation is a barrier and the cross is a stumbling block. The purpose of God is realized only in the pure of heart, who by the enlightenment of the Spirit are able to penetrate the veil and to see in the Man called Jesus something more than a man: the veritable God of gods. Hence our Lord was always asking what people thought of Him. "Whom do men say that I am?" And when His disciples told Him, He pressed them for their own views: "But who do you say I am?" And when Simon Peter gave expression to their belief that He was the Christ, the Son of the living God, Jesus said that he was blessed, for flesh and blood had not revealed this to him. These men associated with Christ daily; yet it took a revelation from on high to cause them to perceive who He was.

So it is to this day. It is possible for a man to be brought up in the church, to be able to quote the Bible with great facility, to be familiar with Christian doctrine and liturgy and yet not accept this truth on which everything else is built. "What do you think of Christ?"—this is the all-important question that divides the world into those who are God's people and those who are not. The truth of His person continues to be believed by some, rejected by others.

St. Paul prayed for the Corinthians that their "faith might be built not upon human wisdom but upon the power of God. And yet," he goes on, "I do speak words of wisdom to those who are ripe for it . . . God's hidden wisdom, His secret purpose framed from the very beginning to bring us to our full glory. The powers that rule the world have never known it; if they had, they would not have crucified the Lord of glory. But in the words of Scripture, 'Things beyond our seeing, things beyond our hearing, things beyond our imagining, all prepared by God for those who love Him,' these it is that God has revealed to us through the Spirit. For the Spirit explores everything, even the depths of God's own nature. . . . A man who is unspiritual refuses what belongs to the Spirit of God; it is folly to him; he cannot grasp it, because it needs to be judged in the light of the Spirit. . . . For (in the words of Scripture) 'who knows the mind of the Lord? Who can advise Him?' We, however, possess the mind of Christ."

Why am I saying all this to you? Chiefly because we modern men need to recapture that sense of reverence, that feeling of awe and wonder that has been characteristic of the church in her best days. We don't have much of it left, because we have discovered so much and invented and explored so much that we have got the notion that we can in time come to know everything and to do anything. Yet we really can know and do nothing without humility; without this virtue we cannot even be people who are acceptable to our fellows, to say nothing of God.

The wise man knows he is continually surrounded and confronted by the most profound mysteries, and of these the greatest is God Himself. Hence we learn reverence first of all in the church. The children in our schools are instructed to come into the church without a sound, since before God we do not babble to one another of our inconsequential concerns but are silent before His majesty, "lost," as one of our hymns puts it, "in wonder, love, and praise." Moses finding himself in the presence of God at the burning bush was instructed to take off his shoes from his feet, for the place on which he was standing was holy ground. So too in our worship we need to have some consciousness of the holiness of Him before whom we stand. He is not like the man next door, and He is something more than "the Man Upstairs." Yet He became our Brother and so is nearer to us than hands or feet. He is above us and in us; one of us yet not one of us; both God and man.

"Great beyond all question is the mystery of our religion: He . . . was manifested in the body." With this sense of mystery, a mystery revealed to us by His Spirit, with this secret in our hearts we can go out of the church into the world, carrying with us a great thankfulness for the wonders that God has made known to us. We can then with new eyes see Him everywhere: in mountains and lakes and trees and birds and fish, in coal and iron and uranium, in the human body and in the souls of His people. "He is not far from every one of us, for in Him we live and move and have our being."

The Mystery of the Church

Ephesians 3:9-10: ". . . the plan of the mystery hidden for ages in God . . . that through the church the manifold wisdom of God might now be made known. . . ."

It might be well to summarize first of all what has been said thus far in this series of sermons. We have defined Christian mystery as a secret that has been revealed, a hidden thing made known. We have said that this action, far from eliminating the element of mysteriousness, only serves to enhance it by deepening the awe and adoration of the beholder and believer. We have pointed out that one comes at these revealed secrets only by faith and that to the unbelieving they are more impenetrable mysteries than ever. And we have always come back to the central mystery of Christianity, from which all the rest derive, which is Jesus Christ, God manifest in the flesh. For it is in Christ that we see God revealed, yet at the same time God hides Himself behind the veil of human flesh. Hence it is necessary to believe that behind this exterior appearance there is a divine reality, that indeed the ineffable Lord is present. These things are true also of that mystery we propose to think about at this time.

There are so many things to be noted under this heading that all I can do is preach a kind of bare-bones sermon, leaving it to another time or to your own study and meditation to supply flesh and sinews to the skeleton.

First off then, the church is the mystery of the divine

life in this world. This is the meaning of St. Paul's metaphor that the church is the body of Christ. Christ, as we have said, is the veritable incarnation of God in the world of men; if this is not so, Christianity has no point and the Gospel has no meaning. Incarnation "denotes the Word becoming flesh and dwelling among us"; that's the primary mystery. Well, this Word, by which we now mean none other than our Lord Jesus Christ, has now assumed another body, which some theologians have referred to as the "extension of the Incarnation." This body is the church, the people in whom God lives and among whom and through whom Christ continues to function as Prophet, Priest, and King. The mysterious part of this is that the presence of God in His church is not as obvious as some might wish it to be. To the outsider the church appears to be a group of people gathered together for the purposes of education, fellowship, moral improvement, and the fostering of works of mercy. What escapes observation is the hidden life of God in the church.

This life begins ordinarily with Holy Baptism. In a way this sacrament is the most mysterious of all churchly acts, because on the face of it nothing seems to happen except the application of water to a human body. Yet the Scriptures urge us to look behind this visible action, assuring us that God Himself is present, incorporating another man into the ongoing life of Christ's body. One becomes a member of this living body by Baptism; this is the being born of water and of the Spirit of which our Lord spoke to Nicodemus. Birth is always a wonderful process, and this is certainly true of this regeneration, which marks one's entrance into the kingdom of God. It's not something one can see at a baptism; yet if our Lord had not instituted this sacrament, there would be nothing to see at all. As always, there is something evident to the senses, something that both reveals and conceals the invisible reality. One must simply accept on faith the proposition that here God is really at work, bringing man to Himself.

A few years ago President Johnson's daughter became a Roman Catholic and was rebaptized upon her admission into that denomination. It seemed to be generally agreed at the time that "somebody goofed." For Holy Baptism is never the sign of one's joining a denomination but always an incorporation into the one church of Jesus Christ. Of course, if your definition of the church is the company of those that are obedient to the Roman pontiff, there may be some justification for what was done by the Washington priest. But a lot of people had been hoping that Rome had become broader than that.

To the church belong those who believe in Christ and have been baptized. This is the New Testament definition, and we stick with it. Those who do not really believe but are only listed as belonging to some particular parish, such are not in the church at all according to the New Testament. Only the faithful are members of the body of Christ; this confronts each of us with the question of whether in fact we are believers and true churchmen. The parable of the weeds among the wheat haunts us: What if our religion should turn out to be made of the stuff to be thrown into the fire at the last day? How can we be sure of being saved from the wrath to come? Are we really in the church, or is ours only an ersatz faith?

This much surely can be said for our comfort: The life that we have in Christ is God's life, not our own. If it were our job to create and sustain it, our situation would certainly be hopeless; we "cannot by our own reason or strength believe in Jesus Christ or come to Him." So we must rely on the Holy Spirit for this, who "would have all men to be saved and to come to the knowledge of the truth." He is serious in His saving purpose. He is active, and He is real. He has made us members of the Christian family by baptism, and He will never repudiate this covenant. Since then by the Word He has brought us to a more mature and informed faith. He has sought to strengthen us in Holy Communion. What this adds up to is that God is bent on our salvation, and He is not entirely frustrated in His loving intention. The thing we need to pray about is our tendency to say no to Him—and this should really concern us.

It is important in this connection that we gear ourselves into the prayer life of the church. The holy conversation with God, which is the church's "vital breath," has been in progress for centuries, and while there have been many variations in the pattern of prayer, there have been some features of it which have been pretty standard. First, definite times and places. The universal experience of Christian people is that unless they tie themselves down to praying at set times and in specific places, the likelihood is that they will not pray at all. As for place, what better one could there be than the church? The recommended times are morning and evening. The idea of the reformers was that the faithful would come together daily in their parish churches for Matins and Vespers. Since under modern conditions this is impossible, or at least highly unlikely, a second best is to say morning and evening prayers wherever we are.

This, according to the mind of the church, would include one or more psalms, a section of Scripture (a table of lessons is printed in the hymnal), a Canticle, the Collect for the week, and whatever other prayers seem appropriate, including the Our Father. These elements are the stuff of which Matins and Vespers are made, and he who would remain in "the fellowship of the mystery" will in this manner pray as the church prays. Timely intercessions and thanksgivings will of course be spoken, for a Christian is always mindful of his priestly obligation to pray for those who stand in need of his prayers. So the mysterious power of God is involved, sometimes with startling results.

The highest and best prayer of the church is the Holy Eucharist. Christians dare not afford to be negligent about their participation in this, even though they might be careless in their daily prayers. For it is in the Eucharist that the mystery of the church comes into prominence as at no other time and in no other way. We have said that the central Christian mystery is that of God, who is pure spirit, coming among men "clothed in our poor flesh and blood." Well, in the Sacrament of the Altar Christ's body and blood are made present and available to us in, with, and under the bread and wine. So, as always, God hides Himself at the same time that He transmits Himself.

> No ear may hear His coming,
> But in this world of sin,
> Where meek folks will
> Receive Him still,
> The dear Christ enters in.

It is because of our awareness of this mystery that we say and do certain things in the liturgy. For instance, we kneel down when we ask Christ to come among us in the Sacrament, and so to bless us with Himself that we might be "filled with heavenly benediction and grace." We sing the great chant of adoration called the Sanctus, uniting our hearts and voices with "all the company of heaven." We bow before His sacramental presence and sign ourselves with the sign of the cross by way of joyful and thankful acknowledgment of our status as redeemed children of God. We also sing some hymns like St. Thomas Aquinas' famous lines:

> Therefore we before Him bending
> This great Sacrament revere.

Or his other hymn:

> Humbly I adore Thee,
> Verity unseen,
> Who Thy glory hidest
> 'Neath these shadows mean;
> Lo, to Thee surrendered,
> My whole heart is bowed,
> 'Tranced as it beholds Thee
> Shrined within the cloud.

Or Bishop Heber's simple but powerful words:

> Bread of the world, in mercy broken,
> Wine of the soul, in mercy shed,
> By whom the words of life were spoken
> And in whose death our sins are dead. . . .

In words like these the church seeks to express her awe and wonder at the sacramental mystery. But associated with this is always corresponding mystery, the mystery of the church herself. St. Augustine spoke of this when he told his people, "You are that which you receive, namely, the body of Christ." For this reason we pray in the Eucharistic Prayer that the Holy Spirit might fill us with Himself, so that we might be indwelt by God. Receiving Holy Communion is God's coming into us, so that our bodies and souls become the hosts of Christ, the mystery thus being consummated in ourselves.

Thus all that we have said ceases to be abstract, speculative, ethereal, and becomes a very personal, intimate, and real association between Christ and ourselves. Here the Bridegroom comes, here the union takes place, here God once more visits His people. "The tabernacle of God is with men," and this tabernacling certainly does not occur apart from the church. This is what many people overlook when they think of the church as a school or a lecture hall or a social club or a humanitarian society and fail to see the great truth that the church is the habitation of God. It is true, of course, that many of us who belong to the church are pretty shabby Christians, and none of us lives up to our profession of faith as we should, but this is precisely the wonder of God's love, that He deigns to dwell among and in people like us.

So we keep on imploring those that are without to look beneath the surface of things and not to judge the church by the tarnished lives of its people but to keep in mind that this is God's way of doing things: to enter this world of men with all its dirt and sin and death in order to redeem it and purify it, first of all to "sanctify and cleanse the church with the washing of water by the Word." Whatever may be said about the church's weaknesses and failures, she is still God's church, still very much alive after nineteen hundred years and destined to continue until she becomes the Church Triumphant. If she were only a human organization, she would long since have perished under the weight of her own crimes, but she is God's people and Christ's body, and this means that the gates of hell will not prevail against her.

And as for you and me, we should regard it as our most glorious privilege to be associated with her.

The Mystery of the Presence

Matthew 28:20: "I am with you always, to the close of the age."

The subject before us today is one of the most difficult in the entire field of theology. I am not at all sure that this sermon will add a great deal to your appreciation for the Blessed Sacrament, for it concerns something that cannot be adequately expressed in human language. Yet the subject can hardly be avoided in any discussion of Holy Communion, since it has been a major cause for the divisions that have existed in the Western Church for over four hundred years. The disagreements have all revolved around "The Mystery of the Presence."

Discerning Christians have always been aware that something occurs during the celebration of the Blessed Sacrament that does not occur otherwise. It is quite true that our Lord has promised to be present wherever two or three are gathered together in His name, whether they are assembled to receive the Sacrament or not. There is such a spiritual presence of Christ that is characteristic of all Christian corporate worship and is quite apart from the sacramental presence. There is also the abiding spiritual presence of our Lord in the heart of the individual in fulfillment of Christ's promise: "If any man love Me, he will keep My words; and My Father will love him, and We will come unto him and make Our abode with him." The theo-

43

logical term for this is the mystical union between Christ and the believer.

But neither Christ's presence among a worshiping congregation nor His indwelling in the soul of the Christian is sufficient to explain the mystery of the presence in the Blessed Sacrament. For it is obvious that in the course of the service something happens that does not happen otherwise. We start out with a quantity of bread and wine, and we believe, according to the apostle's words, that they become the communion of the body and blood of Jesus Christ. Those who receive the sacred elements receive not only the bread and wine that lay on the altar at the beginning of the service; they receive something else. So the overwhelming majority of Christians has always believed, and so the Lutheran Church confesses.

If this is not so, the Sacrament has no point. It is difficult to understand what value the solemn eating of bread and drinking of grape juice has for the people of Reformed churches. They, as you know, teach that our Lord is not present in any other way than He is usually present in the company of Christians. They say He is there spiritually only, meaning that He is there in the same manner as when people assemble to hear the Word and to pray. Why then eat and drink the bread and grape juice? According to Reformed doctrine, this is simply a reminder of the offering of Christ's body and blood on the cross; the action serves to recall the Savior's death on Calvary.

But this surely may be done in other ways: by erecting a cross in front of the church, by showing a picture of the crucifixion, by witnessing a dramatization of the Passion, by singing a Lenten hymn or hearing a Lenten sermon or praying a Litany of the Passion. The use of bread and wine

44

thus becomes one of several devices that may be employed to achieve the same effect; it loses any special significance it might have; it no longer retains the full meaning which our Savior evidently intended it to have when He instituted the Sacrament in the Upper Room. It becomes simply a memorial. But there are various other memorials.

All this may be said in addition to the clear words of St. Paul: "The cup of blessing which we bless, is it not the communion of the blood of Christ? The bread which we break, is it not the communion of the body of Christ?" The Reformed churches do not believe this, because they say it is impossible. Zwingli, Luther's Swiss opponent in this matter, pointed out that the body of Christ, and of course His blood too, had ascended into heaven in the sight of the disciples and that the angel had said He would not return until Judgment Day. We confess in the Creed, said Zwingli, that Christ is now seated at the right hand of the Father. How then is it possible that He should be present in the Sacrament of the Altar? Luther admitted the intellectual difficulty but reminded Zwingli that this was nevertheless the teaching of Scripture. Christ had said: "This is My body," and even though the church could not understand how this might be, she was nevertheless bound to accept it. In other words, we are confronted here with a mystery. And the Christian attitude toward a mystery is not to explain it away but to believe it and wonder at it.

One of the mysteries of the faith, then, concerns the Real Presence of our Lord in the Blessed Sacrament. We have to do here with a miracle. Only we must beware of multiplying miracles so as to believe in a material change of the bread and wine, as the Romanists do. The Roman Church, impressed by the idea that something happens in the course of the Communion service, has attempted to define both the exact moment of the happening and the mode of it. This is something the early church always hesitated to do; it is well to remember that the theory of transubstantiation was not officially accepted until the Lateran Council of 1215 — rather late in the day for a new doctrine to be formulated. This doctrine, aside from its theological niceties, says broadly that the bread and wine lose their substance and are changed into the body and blood of Christ and that this occurs at the moment of consecration.

Non-Roman churches have always contended that this is going entirely too far. The Lutheran Church has argued that the theory does not square with the words of St. Paul, who speaks of bread being distributed and eaten. She furthermore says that we are dealing here with a mystery, not with a problem in philosophy. There is no doubt that Christ comes to His people in a special, sacramental manner, but to say that He does so at a precise moment in the service has no warrant in Holy Scripture. Nor is there any Biblical basis for asserting that He does so by causing the bread to cease being bread and the wine wine. This, however, does not trouble the Church of Rome, which claims to have other and higher authorities than Scripture.

The only thing that can be said with certainty is that each communicant receives the true body and blood of our Lord Jesus Christ. For the rest, the advice of the hymnist is very much in order:

> Search not how this takes place,
> This wondrous mystery;

God can accomplish vastly more
Than seemeth plain to thee.

The truth of the Real Presence, however, must not be held as if our Lord were physically present. Christians are not cannibals; they do not eat the physical body and drink the physical blood of the Lord. If this were so, the source would long ago have been quite exhausted; Christians in the first year after Pentecost would have completely consumed the entire body and all of the blood. Our Savior is present in another way. There is His physical body, which, as Zwingli rightly said, is at the right hand of the Father. There is His mystical body, which is the Church. And there is His sacramental body, present in the Eucharist. This possibly does not make matters any clearer; it is said only to dispel any notion of our eating flesh and drinking blood as certain primitive tribes in the South Seas might do. Our Lord is sacramentally present, not physically. He will not be with us physically until after the Resurrection.

However, if we wish to find illustrations for the sacramental presence, illustrations of our Lord's intention to be really present with His own to the end of time, we must go back to the forty days of Eastertide, to the occasions on which the risen Christ was physically present with His disciples. We must say something like this:

Just as the disciples were assembled in the Upper Room in Jerusalem on Easter evening, so are we assembled here today; and just as the Lord came and stood in their midst, saying, "Peace be unto you," so He now comes among us through the bread and wine, saying through His minister, "The peace of the Lord be with you alway." A prayer in the Mozarabic liturgy gives expression to this thought: "Be present, be present, O good High Priest, as Thou wast in the midst of Thy disciples."

Or we might say that as the Lord Jesus was known to the Emmaus disciples in the breaking of bread, so similarly He is known to us. And we might add that as He was not recognized by them until their eyes were opened, so He is not apprehended by us without the sight of faith.

Or we might say that as the fishermen of Galilee recognized the Lord by the breakfast He had prepared for them on the shore and by His invitation, "Come and dine," so He is perceived by us in the age-old breakfast of the Christian church, to which He regularly and earnestly invites us.

In brief, the forty days of Eastertide have always been regarded as the most blessed days of the church year largely because they were the prototype of the abiding Presence down through the ages. Every celebration of Holy Communion is a kind of extension of those days. He is with us always, even to the end of the world.

Since these things are so, the church seeks to teach us reverence for this holy act by suggesting certain physical acts, like bowing and kneeling, as well as appropriate prayers. It is, for example, traditional to kneel for the Sanctus and to continue so until the distribution. This practice has fallen into disuse among us. We have, however, generally retained the practice of kneeling to receive Communion, as well as bowing both before and after receiving. It is also our custom to kneel for a post-Communion private prayer, to which might well be added the parallel practice of kneeling for a pre-Communion prayer.

Such customs are evidence of the reverence with which the church has ever regarded this sacred mystery. She is careful to guard it against profanation by excluding, as well as she can, those who are known to be ineligible. Manifest and impenitent sinners are advised that they must first repent and make amends. People who are apparently at variance with their fellows are advised to be reconciled with their brethren before they come to the altar. In some churches a special previous confessional service is held for those who have registered for participation in the Communion. These policies are not designed to produce a fear of unworthy reception but are done only because of the holiness of the sacramental Christ. Although Holy Communion is not a thing to be shunned, neither is it something to be taken lightly. We are confronted with a mystery and a miracle. In a very real, special sense we are made partakers of the divine life. We approach that life with joyful expectancy and with humble adoration. We make our preparations, in both body and soul, as thoroughly as possible, for we are to be made one with the ever-living Savior. Christ is with us always; He will be with us now in the Sacrament.

Let all mortal flesh keep silence,
    and stand with fear and trembling
And ponder within itself no earthly thing;
For the King of kings and Lord of lords cometh
To give Himself to be the Food of the faithful.
And before Him come also the angelic hosts
    with all dominion and power,
The many-eyed cherubim and the six-winged seraphim
Covering their faces and crying aloud
    the song, Alleluia.

Thus the liturgy of St. John Chrysostom puts it in a way that could hardly be improved upon. Our privilege in the Sacrament is as near to Isaiah's and St. John's experience as we are likely to get in this life. You remember with what overpowering wonder those prophets of old saw their vision of the Lord Jesus Christ. It is the same Christ who comes among us today. The only difference is in the mode. Let us pray and promise in the words of the Liturgy of St. Basil: "Of Thy sacramental feast this day, O Son of God, accept me as a partaker. I will not give Thee a kiss like Judas, but like the thief I will confess Thee. Remember me, O Lord, in Thy kingdom."

The Mystery of the Cross

**1 Corinthians 1:23-24: "All we preach is Christ cruci-
fied, a stumbling block to the Jews and sheer nonsense
to the Gentiles, but for those who are called, whether
Jews or Greeks, Christ the power of God and the wisdom of God."**

I have seen a painting of Jesus as a young man in the
carpenter shop at Nazareth standing with arms outstretched
and the light from the window behind Him throwing a
shadow in the form of a cross on the sunlit floor. This is
to say that the shadow of the cross was with Him from the
beginning, so that the passage from His birth, which we
considered in an earlier sermon, to His suffering and death,
which is before us now, is a way that we have traveled many
times before; the Incarnation and the Atonement are two
chapters of the same Gospel. It is difficult to say which is
the greater mystery.

Susan K. Langer speaks of the cross as "the actual
instrument of Christ's death, hence a symbol of suffering;
first laid on His shoulders, an actual burden, as well as an
actual product of human handiwork, and on both grounds
a symbol of His accepted moral burden; also an ancient
symbol of the four zodiac points, with a cosmic connotation; a 'natural' symbol of crossroads (we still use it on our
highways before an intersection), and therefore of decision,
crisis, choice; also of being crossed, i.e., of frustration,
adversity, fate; and finally, to the artistic eye a cross is the

figure of a man. All these and many other meanings lie dormant in that simple, familiar, significant shape. No wonder that it is a magical form! It is charged with meanings, all human and emotional and vaguely cosmic, so that they have become integrated into a connotation of the whole religious drama — sin, suffering, and redemption."

Another author suggests that the cross represents a crossroads extending toward four fronts: "backward toward the past; forward into the future; inward among ourselves, our feelings, wishes, and dreams; and outward against what we must fight or exploit or come to terms with or ignore. It is obviously fatal to fail on any front. Yet it is equally obvious that no individual can move adequately in all four directions at once. Therefore life is perpetual decision. . . ."

All this is quite true, and yet it does not come at the central mystery of the cross, which is the atoning sacrifice of the Lamb of God. Neither of these writers says anything about Him who hung on the cross, and one would think that they would, since He is the meaning of the symbol. The cross is nothing without Christ! Whoever wishes to penetrate into the mystery of the cross must know something of the Crucified One. On the other hand, Christ cannot be understood apart from His cross. The whole purpose of His coming reached its climax there. This is supremely what He came to do: to give His life as a ransom for many. The Savior and His cross go together.

The base of the cross was driven into the earth, but the top of it points to the heavens. This is to say, the crucifixion occurred at a particular time and place and yet has eternal significance. We say on the one hand that our Savior was crucified under Pontius Pilate, which is the church's way of dating the event; but on the other hand people have been saying for sixteen hundred years that this thing was done "for us men and for our salvation" — and they will probably still be saying it at the end of time. So what happened once avails always, and this is so because not only men were involved in this historical incident, but God was, who is the timeless One. The vertical beam of the cross points upward, and most of the seven words of the Crucified were directed to Him who dwells in the heavens.

Christ Himself was both God and man. As man He could be nailed to a piece of wood dropped into a hole in the ground; as God He could bring the perfect sacrifice necessary for the redemption of the world. We need to hold both things in balance in our thinking and believing.

If the Crucified One is only a man, then this story is but one of the many tragedies of which history is full, an outstanding example of a miscarriage of justice, but nothing more; one instance among many of the failure of mankind to appreciate its prophets and saints. But this certainly gives us no comfort. If the church's teaching about the deity of Christ be not true, we are not reconciled with God, and our Lenten devotions are pointless.

If on the other hand the Crucified One be only God and not man — but this obviously is not so, because He had a back that was beaten, a head that was crowned with thorns, and hands and feet that were pierced with nails. He was man all right; He was representative Man, the second Adam, the embodiment of the whole human race; He was mankind. Thus it is rightly said that we were crucified *with* Him and are buried *with* Him by baptism into death. He identified Himself with us, so that we might be identified with Him in His sacrifice.

The downward and upward movement of Christ and His Father is continually being negated by the crossbeam of human iniquity. What Christ is is denied. What He wishes to do is resisted. His love is met with hatred, His Word with denial, His sacrifice with rejection. He comes to His own, and His own receive Him not. His Gospel is put down as foolishness, indeed, as opium for the people. As men crucified His physical body, so they try to exterminate His mystical body, the church.

Why do people behave this way? Can they not see that this is the most sublime message ever heard, that God's purpose is to bless them with an indescribable blessing, that their whole temporal and eternal welfare is bound up with their acceptance or rejection of Christ? Why are they so perverse as to do things that are detrimental to their own welfare?

There is no other answer to this except the doctrine of original sin. Unpleasant though it may be, the fact of the matter is that we are by nature blind, dead, and enemies of God. Anyone who is disinclined to believe this is referred to the story of the crucifixion. There you have proof of it. There is human perversity in all its ugliness, hatefulness, and satanic intensity. This is what sinful man is capable of: killing the Prince of life, murdering the Son of God. So with one crushing blow the crossbeam smashes all sentimental notions of the essential goodness of man, the teaching that we need only to be educated; that once we have been shown what is good, we will adopt it and follow it.

J. B. Priestley in a broadcast talk some years ago described his visit to the bombed-out cathedral at Coventry. "In some such roofless glowing place," he said, "the early

Christians might have worshipped. Only not with so many memories. For there in that ruin of a once magnificent church stood a large black cross, made out of charred wood, and carved in the stone beneath it were two simple words, 'Father, forgive.' And outside in the streets they were selling the papers that told the same old story of indifference, drift, mischief, prejudice, passion, and blind idiocy."

A good illustration this is of the contrast between God's way with man and man's way with God. God deals with us in such a way that it is "a stumbling block to the Jews and sheer nonsense to the Gentiles," because it is the way of service, surrender, and sacrifice, the way of redeeming love. Man's way is the opposite: the way of self-assertion, dominance over others, the way of greed and power and violence. Man despises God's way, and God is always trying to change man's ways, and the conflict comes to a head in the cross. God's way is such a reproach to man's ways that man is stirred to commit deicide, thinking to silence the voice that calls him, to put out of the way the Person who summons him to repentance and faith. But it's no good. The cross still stands in Coventry Cathedral as it does all over the world, and beyond it is the Christ over whom death has no more dominion.

This brings us to the other half of the text, in which St. Paul says that "for those who are called, whether Jews or Greeks, Christ [is] the power of God and the wisdom of God." Here is the real mystery of the cross, which becomes so evident in those who see it as the instrument of their redemption. Its mysteriousness lies in a number of paradoxes, which may be stated as follows:

First, the crucifixion of Jesus was so monstrous a crime

that no worse thing can be said about man than that man is capable of doing *that;* yet the cross of Christ has elevated and dignified man more than any other influence in history. We know this because we see that everywhere in the world, wherever the cross has been raised, man has been raised to a new nobility. Man becomes the creature for whom Christ died, on whom the Father has set His love, in whom the Lord and Giver of life has begun to work.

It is said that the humanist scholar Muretus, in the sixteenth century, a fugitive from France, fell ill in Lombardy and, looking like a vagabond in rags, asked aid of the doctors. The physicians discussed his case in Latin, thinking that this bedraggled pauper could not understand the learned tongue. "Faciamus experimentum in anima vili," they said: "Let us try an experiment with this worthless creature." And to their amazement the "worthless creature" spoke to them in Latin: "Will you call worthless one for whom Christ did not disdain to die?" The influence of this idea has been incalculable. It is responsible for practically all charitable endeavor in the world today, for behind it is a respect for human personality in even its most wretched forms. And this respect comes from the Crucified One, whose sacrifice forever testifies to the value of man.

The second paradox is that the cross was a crushing defeat of righteousness and yet was the greatest victory that righteousness ever won. What an amazing thing, that throughout Christendom in these next two weeks we shall be celebrating the most colossal failure in all history! What a strange practice, that whenever Christians bring forth bread and wine in their churches they show forth the Lord's death! What an odd custom to set up the cross, the instrument of an execution, in the most prominent places we can think of! The explanation, of course, is that Christ, being raised from the dead, dies no more; it is nevertheless interesting, to say the least, that the most prominent symbol of Christianity is not of the resurrection but of the death of Christ.

One reason for this must be that we, who are still in the Church Militant, are embroiled in constant struggle, and the cross is the epitome of struggle. It was there, on Golgotha, that the powers of evil did their utmost to rob of His righteousness the embodiment of all that was good. How did they not taunt Him there to come down from the cross, to save Himself, to give the whole thing up as an insane idea! This they did when, because of His physical torment and His mental anguish, He was as vulnerable as a human being could be. And they failed! The worst they could do was not enough to get Him off the track. He said no to it all. He retained His integrity. He won!

This is why the cross says so much to us struggling human beings. For certainly we grow weary and are frequently tempted to throw in the towel. But the cross says to us that there is something in the world stronger and deeper than the things that succeed, namely, the things that fail, the things that are right and that honorably and sacrificially fail. Surrender to the will of God and service to mankind are the things that finally are victorious. This is why George Tyrell, a brave soul fighting a hard battle for the truth against many enemies, once wrote: "Again and again I have been tempted to give up the struggle, but always the figure of that strange Man hanging on the cross sends me back to my task again." He does that every Sunday, does He not, and whenever during the week we think of Him. The cross preaches to us the potency of a life that cares enough about man to die for him. And "if it die, it bringeth forth much fruit."

The final paradox is this: The cross was a denial of God; yet it was supremely the revelation of God. We spoke before about the unbelieving hostility of man; we speak now of what God has wrought. We can speak of this because, to us who are called, Christ is the Power of God and the Wisdom of God — Power because He has made new men of us, Wisdom because in the cross and resurrection we can penetrate into the deepest mysteries of life and death. Certainly we do not know all the answers. We do not understand the problem of suffering, for example, but even in deepest suffering we can cling to the unshakable fact of God's love as revealed in the cross of our Savior. This is how He feels about us, this is what He has done for us; come what may, these things stand fast. What does a man have who does not have this when the time of tribulation comes?

Well does the Introit for Passion Sunday, after it has spoken of ungodly nations and deceitful and unjust men, say to the Lord for us all: "Thou art the God of my strength. Oh, send out Thy light and Thy truth; let them lead me, let them bring Me to Thy holy hill!" Thank God that there is such a strength, such light, and such truth and that God does by them bring us at last to Himself.

The Mystery of Death and Resurrection

2 Timothy 1:10: " [He] abolished death and brought life and immortality to light through the Gospel."

On Easter Day in the year 627 King Edwin of Northumbria was baptized by Paulinus of York. In his *Church History of the English Nation* the Venerable Bede reports the proceedings of the council at which the king and his advisers decided to seek Baptism. This is the oft-quoted speech made by one of the chieftains on that occasion:

> Your Majesty, when we compare man's present life with the time about which we know nothing, it seems to me to resemble the swift flight of a solitary sparrow through the banquet-hall where you sit dining with your thanes and councilors during the winter months. Inside there is a comforting fire that warms the room, while outside winter snowstorms and rainstorms are raging. This sparrow flies in quickly through one door of the hall, and then flies out through another. While he is inside, he is safe from the winter storms, but after a few comfortable moments he disappears into the darkness from which he has come. In the same way, man appears for a little while on earth, but of what went before this life and of what is to follow we know nothing. Therefore, if this new teaching has some more certain knowledge to reveal, it seems only right for us to follow it.

This may serve as an introduction to our subject.

We call death a mystery because no one of us has experienced it, nor has any of us talked with someone who has returned from it. There is no communication with the spirits of those who have died; the claims of the spiritualist and spiritist groups have been repeatedly exposed as fakery and quackery. Death is a closed door, and whatever may be on the other side of it is hid from our sight and hearing. Through the long history of mankind all sorts of speculations have been made, and even whole religions, like that of ancient Egypt, have centered in the state of the dead, but all these have been nothing more than human surmises; no one has had any reliable information whatsoever. Death has remained a mystery.

Probably the noblest of all pagan views of death is expressed in Plato's famous description of the death of Socrates, who in complete equanimity said farewell to his friends, spoke to them of the meaning of life and death, and then drank the poisonous hemlock and laid himself down to die. For him death was the great liberator, freeing the soul from the prison of the body, so that it might return to its eternal home. Therefore he did not fear death but rather thought of it as the soul's great friend. The immortality of the soul is assumed.

But it is very important to bear in mind that this is a pagan doctrine, which is essentially different from the Christian teaching concerning the resurrection of the body. The Scriptures say plainly that the soul, being sinful, is under the sentence of death, which is the same thing as saying that is has no essential immortality. Our Lord taught us to "fear Him who can destroy both soul and body in hell" — and this does not sound like any automatic translation of departing spirits to a "beautiful isle of somewhere." And our text says that Christ has "brought life and immortality to light"; this means that before Christ and apart from Christ there was and is no immortality. It's a priceless gift which only those who are in Him enjoy. This follows from the fact that He, and only He, is the Conqueror of death.

What happens when a man dies? Quite obviously his body stops functioning. Almost as obviously the process of decay sets in immediately. This is why, in warmer climates and in poorer civilizations, burial takes place the same day as death. ("It's summer, and we're runnin' out of ice.") Our morticians apply temporary preservatives to the corpse and appropriate cosmetics to the face, so that friends may come to the funeral parlor and remark how natural the deceased looks. This is supposed to be comforting; the assumption seems to be that the deceased has now reverted to that health, youth, and vigor which he enjoyed before disease, old age, or evil accident laid him low. And there is always the suggestion, because he has been made to look like that, that he has not died at all, that he will at any moment sit up and begin to speak. But all the while the grim fact of the matter is that the man is dead, that he won't move or speak again, and that in a little while corruption and decay will do its worst in the grave. This is not pleasant, but it is reality.

However, for our blessed Lord there was no bodily decay. "Thou wilt not suffer Thine Holy One to see corruption." It is precisely because He was the Holy One that His body did not see corruption; just as our bodies *will* decay because we are unholy. For this physical disintegration is the result of sin, and since Christ was free of sin, He was exempt from this consequence of it. We are not so exempt, which means that death, far from being the friend Socrates thought it to be, is our greatest enemy. So do the

61

Scriptures speak of it: "The last enemy that shall be destroyed," writes St. Paul, "is death." For death is contrary to the will of God. It tears apart what He has joined together, it destroys His creation. God is the Life-Giver, the Unifier; death effects the breaking up of the living organism He has made. And the revolting disintegration that takes place in the grave is the end product of the corruption that was introduced on the day of the fall.

But more important and dreadful than this is what happens to the soul as the result of sin. We might describe this as the loneliness of man or at least as the rupture of fellowship. This has a vertical and a horizontal direction: it is a break between God and man, and it is a break between man and his fellows. You can see a vivid example of both in the Passion of our Savior. "My God, My God, why hast Thou forsaken Me?" He cried out on the cross, and it was undoubtedly the prospect of this forsakenness that had caused much of His agony in Gethsemane. In that hour He desperately sought the strength of human fellowship, only to find that the three men whom He had most relied on to stand by Him repeatedly fell asleep and seemed to have no understanding at all of what He was going through. Later all eleven of His trusted friends ran away in terror, and only St. John and His mother had the courage to stand under His cross. All the rest who passed by on that dreadful day jeered at Him. Christ in His extremity was left horribly alone. It's a thing that every man feels to some extent and at certain times, and some men feel it all the time: the sense of being all alone in the world, without love from either God or man. And certain it is that when it comes to dying, each of us must do that all by himself; no one else can go through the gates with us.

Death is the breaking of the fellowship between the deceased and his loved ones. This, as every bereaved person knows, is the hardest thing of all: to face up to the fact that the departed person will never speak or respond to us again; there is no association with someone who is dead. So the disciples felt when Christ died, and in their case the dreadful sensation of loss was compounded, for the One who had died was not an ordinary man but He who, as they trusted, was to redeem Israel. Their desolation was therefore great indeed; there seemed to be no future, because there would be no Christ in that future. But then on the third day the ruptured fellowship was restored, and "the disciples were glad when they saw the Lord." I should think they would be! For this was something utterly new, completely different in the history of mankind.

This was not like the resurrection of Lazarus, who was simply restored to his former place and duty and after a while died a second time. Christ was raised to a glorified kind of existence, He was no longer restricted by the ordinary limitations of the body, and, above all else, He will never die again. It was this that so amazed the disciples and, when the full significance and wonder of it had sunk into their souls, made it the constant theme of their preaching. What they were so excited about was not that a certain man named Jesus had by some mysterious legerdemain been restored to life again but rather than death itself had been conquered, death in all its hostile power, its ugliness, its satanic destructiveness, its full horror. God in Christ had actually overcome this monstrous enemy, so that St. Paul can say in the text: "Christ has abolished death."

This, you see, is something quite different from the idea of the immortality of the soul. Oscar Cullman puts the difference this way: "Belief in the immortality of the soul is not belief in a revolutionary event. Immortality, in fact, is only a negative assertion: the soul does not die, but simply lives on. Resurrection is a positive assertion: the whole man, who has really died, is recalled to life by a new act of creation by God. Something has happened — a miracle of creation!" To this we must certainly add that it is the creation of a new kind of man, the kind of man which the disciples saw Christ to be during Eastertide.

Now to come back for a moment to the apostle's assertion that Christ has abolished death: does not this overstate the case? It is obvious that people continue to die just as they did before Easter. So what's the difference? The difference is first of all that He whom we call the Lord and Giver of life has since the Day of Pentecost been making a ceaseless invasion into the domain of death. He establishes a new bridgehead every time a human being is incorporated into the ongoing life of Christ, just as, on the physical side, He wins another victory whenever a disease is conquered and whenever a sufferer is healed. In these ways death is constantly pushed back; indeed, in our day physical death has been made to retreat so far that we are hard pressed to know what to do with all the human life that is being produced.

However, at the last all men must die, a little later than they did formerly but inevitably still. What has God done about this? He has made it possible, for as many as will lay hold of His gift by faith, for any man to die in the confidence that the same thing will happen to him as happened to his Lord. There will indeed by physical decay, but there will also be a restoration and a glorification and a life everlasting. There will be a fellowship with Christ and His saints that will never be broken and will continue on a plane impossible for us now. There will in this situation be a complete abolition of death and all its painful preliminaries. There will be immortality, not in the Greek but in the Christian sense, as a priceless gift which the redeemed will enjoy in Christ. All this is admittedly in the future, but so sure and certain is it that the apostle can use the past tense and say, "Christ has abolished death."

Thus it is that the mystery of death has been made less mysterious by the resurrection of Jesus Christ. The secret has been revealed, the problem solved, the enemy overcome, the terror removed. Christians do not fear death, for as Paul says, not even this can separate us from the love of Christ. Those who have died in the Lord are blessed and peacefully await the most resounding blessing of all, when the trumpet shall sound and we shall be raised incorruptible. There remains, of course, the rupture of fellowship which death effects, but we know this is only temporary and that the kind of association we shall enjoy come Resurrection Day will be far superior to anything within the present range of our experience.

These things we celebrate every Sunday, which is always a little Easter. We associate them with our Baptism, which is a participation in Christ's death and resurrection. And we are involved in them in every Eucharist, which is several things at once: a making present and available the sacrificial death of our Savior, a communion with the living Lord, and a fellowship with one another in the sacramental Christ, which is a foretaste of our eating and drinking new in the Father's kingdom of glory. By these things the church lives and moves forward to their consummation on the day of Christ's return.

Crossroads

By George F. Lobien

Preface

The sermons you have in hand are very much the personal witness of the author. They disclose how I understand God to be working in contemporary life. Although intended originally for lay people with whom I lived and worshiped, the material, I believe, can be meaningful to clergy as well.

Some of the subjects treated are such that there are no direct Scriptural parallels. Pollution and population control were not items of significant importance to first-century Christians. Today they are meaningful issues to which the church must address itself. Although there are no Bible passages dealing directly with these topics, many sections of Scripture are applicable.

These sermons were written out of the conviction that the crucifixion, resurrection, and ascension of Jesus have significance to all of life. They proclaim the message that the redemption accomplished by Christ was so radical and complete that it frees us from sin's burden and opens to us the possibility of being a blessing not only to God's people but to all mankind. Our aim is to emphasize the practical value of our Lord's self-giving on behalf of His body, the church. (Col. 1)

GEORGE F. LOBIEN

Crossroads

Dear Father, the cross of Your Son occupies a central position in most of our church buildings. Grant that our lives may be as Christian as our architecture. In Christ's name we pray. Amen.

You can buy it at a jewelry store with a diamond center for twelve hundred dollars, or you can purchase it at a dime store for nineteen cents. You might find it in the pocket of a fox-holed GI or dangling from the neck of a prizefighter. Sometimes it is made of metal, but it could be constructed of wood or of plastic that glows in the dark. I have seen it formed by neon lights. It used to be a secret sign hastily scratched in the sand and quickly erased with the sandal. It gets tattooed on sailors, and the chests of clergy often sport it laden with precious gems. Who could count the sizes, shapes, and forms in which it comes or how many copies of it have been produced since the first century? How often has it been mentioned in literature? How many hymns contain reference to it? You know of what I speak: The Cross.

The cross of Jesus Christ is more popular than the Eisenhower jacket, the Wright Brothers' airplane, or the Ringling Brothers' Circus. It is more widely recognized than such national shrines as the Statue of Liberty or the Eifel Tower. The cross has come a long way since its invention.

Perhaps the cross was first used as an instrument of

punishment and death by the Phoenicians and the Persians. Of that we cannot be certain. But we do know for sure that it was adopted by the Romans as a savage means of executing slaves and foreigners. Those who were raised up on it were first humiliated by being forced to carry the means of their own destruction, at least the transverse part of it, to the place of execution. Then they were stripped and elevated for the abuse of all. To the Jew the cross was a public demonstration of servitude to the Roman overlord.

When you stop to think about it, the cross is quite an insignia for Christians to follow in procession. Is there no better symbol of our platform? Is there no worthier gesture with which to bless ourselves or others? Would not the civilian salute to the flag be more appropriate? Or what about the sign of the black power party — the raised clenched fist? But we are devoted to the cross because the tradition to which we are heirs is one that proclaims it as central to all that exists in our world.

Perhaps you think I spoke carelessly or overstated my case in what I have just said. Dismiss that thought from your mind. I believe and am persuaded that the cross of Jesus Christ has meaning and consequence for spiritual life and for physical life, for nature and for the course of history, for politics and for national priorities. If Calvary does not affect all of life *now,* then it had no significant meaning when it happened, and life is a senseless rat race in which we consume while we can until we are eventually consumed by a hostile environment of our own creation.

But Christian theology claims that the life and death of Jesus Christ is central to all existence. Paul boldly says of Jesus, "He is before all things, and in Him all things hold together." God's ruined and rebellious creation was repaired and rededicated to its Owner by the death of Jesus Christ on a tree hewn by the hand of man. Peace was made between God and creation "by the blood of His cross." (Col. 1:20)

The story is told about an Anglican bishop and his dog. They had shared fourteen years of life with its many ups and downs. When Rex fell asleep for the last time, the bishop buried him in his own plot in the parish cemetery. He even erected a little tombstone in his pet's memory on which were the words: "Here lieth Rex — for whom Romans 8:19 ff. doth afford some slight hope."

For the benefit of the few of you who did not read Romans 8:19 ff. yesterday, allow me to refresh your memory about those verses. In that magnificent portion of Paul's letter to the Romans he proclaimed the universal significance of Christ's life and death by saying that even nature is suffering with us and anxiously awaiting the ultimate reign of Christ. Paul taught that on the final day creation itself would be set free from its bondage to decay and share in our liberation. After all, it was not the flitting birds and the buzzing bees that rebelled against God, yet they were forced to participate in the results of our revolt against the Creator, and they do so to this day. Hence they share in our hope of redemption. Because of the crucifixion the day is coming when one creature will not live by the death of another. We await a time when the insight of Tennyson will not be true. He said, "Of a thousand seeds, she brings forth one."

When the body of Christ was fixed to the cross, the offenses of every man were bound to the tree. A sacrifice of such consequence occurred that nature had reason to hope for deliverance from its bondage to decay (Rom. 8:21).

Even spiritual forces of evil were overcome by that great saving act (Col. 2:14-15). The word about the cross might be foolishness to many, but to those who are in the know it is the power of God (1 Cor. 1:18). The value of the cross cannot be overestimated. Paul said to the Corinthians: "I decided to know nothing among you except Jesus Christ and Him crucified" (1 Cor. 2:2). Those with the insight of faith know that the power of God is more apparent at the crucifixion of His Son than it was when the Savior walked on the water and calmed the storms. The self-sacrifice of Jesus made evident to every man the extent to which God loves and gives for His people. The crucifixion proclaimed in unmistakable terms that the God of creation is also the God of redemption.

As people who share a common heritage and live in the same land, we must be concerned about the fact that our nation stands at the juncture of many crossroads. The intersections are so numerous and so consequential that they befuddle most who do not have the vision to scan the landscape from the vantage point of Calvary. The names on the road signs are simple enough for all to read. They are words like: poverty or plenty; pollution or conservation; population control or indiscriminate breeding; purposeful politics or professional aggrandizement. Those who shield their eyes with rose-colored lenses believe that we can drive down all roads simultaneously, straddling the issues as it were. Some have decided to travel the path of personal pleasure despite the outcome. But those who believe that the cross of Jesus Christ affects all creation will undoubtedly realize that disciples must still take up their crosses, those instruments of self-sacrifice, and follow Jesus.

It was for such a time as ours that Christ lived and died. The cross was the altar upon which the once-for-all sacrifice for mankind was given to God, reconciling our world to the Father (2 Cor. 5:19). The cross of crosses was raised up more than 1,900 years ago, but it still has the power to transform the world because we who live today share in the life that was offered upon it. Through our baptism we share his death, for we were baptized into it (Rom. 6:3). The penalty for our sins was paid in full at Calvary. We are God's people, ransomed by the blood of Jesus. But more than that, we are reborn with Christ for a new life of freedom and power in our world. After the price Christ paid to secure our freedom and to empower us for new life, we cannot afford to live like men bound by imaginary prison bars. The leash of Satan has been cut from our necks. Sin no longer enslaves us (Rom. 6). We can transform our world. Christ gives us the power to do so.

Ours is a nation standing at the crossroads. Thank God we have a cross to raise in the midst of our havoc. Put yourself upon it and be raised high where the sons of God may be lifted up as signs to a confused and bewildered humanity. You are the body of Christ. You belong on a cross at the crossroads. You know the end of your suffering. It will not be in vain! (1 Cor. 9:19-27; 15:58)

Text:

He is the Image of the invisible God, the Firstborn of all creation; for in Him all things were created, in heaven and on earth, visible and invisible . . . all things were created through Him and for Him. He is before all things, and in Him all things hold together. . . . For in Him all the fullness of God was pleased to dwell, and through Him to reconcile to Himself all things, whether on earth or in heaven, making peace by the blood of His cross. (Col. 1:15-19)

Dear Father,
We have all experienced wood.
Most of us have known the sting of a splinter
        piercing our flesh.
But none of us has been so closely bound to wood
        as Your Son
        when men nailed and bound Him to the tree.
For our sins
        His splinters were spikes.
His body felt the grain of wood
        which our eye has often admired
        in its highly polished state.

You loved us, Lord!
And we repent of the fact that our sin made love so
        painful for You and Your well-loved Son.
We thank You for not shirking from the sacrifice that was
        necessary to reclaim all that Your hand created.
We are not sure why it had to be this way,
        but we know that it was necessary
        or You would not have paid such a price for our
        salvation.

It's about the fact that we are expected to take up crosses
        and follow in the footsteps of Your Son
        that we are most concerned.
He was a man like us.
        But we are not sure that we can be men
        like Him.

Thank You for a sacrament, Lord,
   by which we can be forgiven and strengthened.
Thank You for the fellowship of other pilgrims
   who walk in Christ's footsteps with us.
As we have been strengthened by them,
   help us to find a weary soul
   whose burdens we might share or bear.

We know You can use us to be a blessing to others
   because of the all-sufficient sacrifice of Jesus.
Do it, Lord!
   Take our lives and let them be
   Consecrated, Lord, to Thee.
   Amen.

Crossroads: Population

Dear Father, with the gift You have given to create life, give us also the will to do so responsibly, that our actions may confirm our creeds. Hear us for Jesus' sake. Amen.

The opening words of the Apostles' Creed are these: "I believe in God the Father Almighty, Maker of heaven and earth" (*TLH*, p. 12). In a somewhat more expanded form the Nicene Creed similarly confesses: "I believe in one God, the Father Almighty, Maker of heaven and earth and of all things visible and invisible" (*TLH*, p. 22). The Athanasian Creed concerns itself primarily with the concept of the Trinity, but by inference one might claim that it also acknowledges God as Creator when it states of our Lord that He is "God of the Substance of the Father, *begotten before the worlds;* and Man of the substance of His mother, born in the world." (*TLH*, p. 53, emphasis added)

To my mind there is no way to deny the creative activity of God and still remain within the Judeo-Christian tradition. The followers of Christ reaffirmed their commitment to a Creator-God when they relied on Jesus to deal decisively with natural phenomena and when they made confessions such as that found in the Letter to the Hebrews: "By faith we understand that the world was created by the Word of God." (Heb. 11:3)

In saying these things I do not mean to imply that we are bound to the world view of past centuries. In a certain sense it is no longer adequate to confess God as "Maker of heaven and earth." There is much more to creation than heaven and earth. We might fit our space-age cosmology more easily into the Nicene phrase "and of all things visible and invisible."

To my mind many of the crises we face today may be traced to the doorsteps of millions of Christians who have failed to take seriously their theology of creation. Either they have forgotten to confess God as Creator altogether, or they have overestimated the rights and privileges of that which stands at the apex of creation: MAN.

A noted botanist from the University of Wisconsin claims that there are two ways to view man. The one is to accept the thesis that we are but a thin slice of evolution above the apes. The other is to confess that we are but a thin slice of baloney beneath the angels. Both views may be helpful in understanding people and their behavioral patterns, but I will add to the opinions already expressed that man should come to think of himself as a creature who has fallen heir to the image of God in a unique way.

While there is much theological debate over what the phrase "image of God" means, I believe that one of its Old Testament meanings is that man has been given *authority* by God which he is to use *responsibly* toward creation. This appears evident in the second Biblical creation account, in which man was given the responsibility to name all that God created, among which there was nothing that could serve as a helper fit for him, not even the dog. And in the first account of creation the writer says:

"Then God said, 'Let Us make man in Our image, after Our likeness; and let them *have dominion* over the fish

79

of the sea and over the birds of the air and over the cattle and over all the earth and over every creeping thing that creeps upon the earth.' So God created man in His own image, in the image of God He created him; male and female He created them. And God blessed them, and God said to them, 'Be fruitful and multiply, and fill the earth and subdue it; and *have dominion* over the fish of the sea and over the birds of the air and over every living thing that moves upon the earth.' " (Gen. 1:26-28)

But mankind seems not to have understood the intention of God in making us in His image. Many of us rip from their sacred context the words, "Be fruitful and multiply!" as we create and procreate, "doin' what comes naturally." To be entrusted with dominion over all of God's creation is an awesome responsibility.

It occurs to me that in the population explosion of the 20th century man may be rebuilding the tower of Babel, arrogantly assuming that he can use the power of God without restraint. But the "blessing" of God (Gen. 1:28) may not thus be spurned. We Babel builders will soon discover that there are no more fish in the sea and birds in the air and cattle in the fields and creeping things in the earth over which we can exercise dominion — which implies ruling for their benefit — and we will stand face to face with the enemy and realize that it is us.

Most of you know the problem. Basic to the most serious threats faced by our nation today is the "people explosion." In the year 1 A. D. it is estimated that 250,000,000 people lived on earth. It took until 1850 for the population to hit the billion mark. But only eighty years later we had two billion people milling around on the face of the earth. That was in 1930. In just thirty years

80

more (1960) we had passed the three billion total, and today (1971) we have in excess of three and a half billion people living in our world. Current estimates call for a population of approximately seven billion people, twice as many as we have today, by A. D. 2000. Need I remind you that the year 2000 is well within the lifespan of many of you reading this page? By that time, many ecologists believe, environmental and food supply problems will be insurmountable, and another species will be lost to creation — the species *Homo sapiens.*

If this prospect seems frightening to you, let me say that I am not nearly as frightened by the possibility of the extinction of the human race as I am about the way I believe the species *Homo sapiens* will survive.

If we were to put too many apes together in one place, do you know what would happen? There would be famine as the food supply dwindled. There would be fighting as each tried to establish property rights and to provide for physical needs. There would be neuroses as one animal grated on the nerves of another. There would be sickness as epidemics spread rapidly among the dense population. There would be sexual perversion and general loss of reproductive powers. Females would even begin to destroy their young. Are we a thin slice of evolution above the apes?

Look at our world. Is there famine? God knows there is. Is there war and violence? God knows there is. Are instances of neurotic sickness increasing? God knows they are. Is there sexual perversion in our day? Who could deny it? Certainly not I. And though human beings are not prone to destroy their young after birth, the incidents of abortion continue to rise.

Our world, God's creation entrusted to us as stewards,

is being destroyed because we must use unnatural means to feed, clothe, and sustain our physical life. There has come about an unholy alliance between medicine, politics, religion, and egotism that has given us universal death control with a paucity of birth control. And in the meantime many Christians are unwilling to do something about this important issue.

Reverence for life is one excuse advanced by some. At this time in history we must have reverence for the *diversity* of life God has given. Today the question has become: *What* must be destroyed and *who* must go hungry that I and mine may survive? We who live in the United States of America make up only 5.7 percent of the world's population, yet we consume some 40 percent of the world's natural resources. How long shall we continue to pillage and plunder the earth for the sake of our own welfare while our brothers and sisters, who are loved by God as much as we are, must pay for the consequences of our affluence?

When I look at the cross of my Lord Jesus Christ and consider what He sacrificed for our world and for everyone who lives in it, I am filled with shame. There are days when it is difficult for me to admit that I am a member of the human race — that privileged form of life assumed by my Savior that we might have an abundant life in God's world. In place of exercising stewardship over God's blessings to us in nature and in people, we have deserted the Christian virtues of humility, self-sacrifice, and trustworthiness for an attitude of arrogance and indifference. I believe history will show that one of the most tragic failures of the church in our century is its unwillingness to espouse population control. The classic statement of that failure will be Pope Paul's Encyclical on Birth Control. It is easy for us to throw stones because the pontiff's position is on paper, but we Lutherans have also failed to be the sensible leaven we should have been in the light of God's many blessings to us.

Lent is the time the church has set apart for personal introspection. We must examine ourselves, not only as individuals but also as citizens of a nation. After all, the failures of our world are but the failures of each one of us compounded.

Do you love the world like God loved it? After all, it was your sin He bore in His body on the cross! Are you willing to sacrifice for it like God paid the price for its redemption? I hope you are, for I believe it is only the knowledge of God's loving forgiveness and the compelling example of Jesus on a cross that can give us strength to carry the burden now beginning to come upon us. The weight of guilt has been lifted from our shoulders. A light and lively yoke has been prepared for us, a yoke we can carry by the strength Christ gives.

God loves us, dear friends. He loves each one of us despite our selfishness and our indifference. And there lies our hope.

Because Jesus was not only prepared to give up His life for us but actually did commit Himself completely to the Father's will, we can follow in His footsteps. He came among us as a man demonstrating that men are exalted by God when they give of themselves completely in God's service (Phil. 2:4-11). We look not only to our own interests but also to the needs of others (Phil. 2:4) because He served us in total self-sacrifice. And being assured of His victorious resurrection, we know that our labor will not be wasted.

Perhaps the love of God, which stained the wood of the cross and made heroes out of first-century cowards, can work its miracle again. Perhaps we will consent to be lifted up at the crossroads.

Text:

I came that they may have life and have it abundantly. I am the Good Shepherd. The good shepherd lays down his life for the sheep. (John 10:10-11)

Dear Father,
    we praise You for the gift of people.
Made like You in all respects, except with sin,
        we thank You for destroying its power over us and
        for enabling us to do Your will in Your world.
We are not using our creative powers in a creative way,
    O Lord!
We note that over what You created there was a single
    judgment:
        And God saw that it was good!
You have obviously noted that much we have made is
    not good.
We make too much!
We create for the wrong reason!
We deny others that we might have for ourselves!
Save us from our creative sins
    before they blot out our confession
    concerning Your creative genius.
Make us more sensitive to what is involved
    in exercising dominion over Your handiwork.
Help us to understand the creativity of Christ that drove
    Him to a cross.
Just because our crosses are not made of wood, You un-

derstand (do You not?)
   that we need Your strengthening
   as much as Christ did?
Of course You do, O Lord,
   and we rejoice that You have given us Your Son's
   power and the pledge of His presence.
We will use both in honor of Your name
   and for the benefit of those
   for whom our Lord died.
Praise be to You, our Creator-God. Amen.

Crossroads: Politics

Dear Father, we confess that Yours is the controlling interest in human affairs. Let Your will be done through us and among us for Jesus' sake. Amen.

If Monday-morning quarterbacking is America's favorite sport, Monday-morning politicking is not far behind in popularity. "If *I* were President of the United States—" is a famous first line we have probably all thought of at some time or another. It is a pleasing thought because it propels us from the position of anonymity and weakness to one of power and prestige. It is a nonthreatening thought because few, if any of us, will ever have to act on the basis of it. It is safe for us to daydream.

The problem with such thinking, however, is that it can subconsciously become the basis for a lethargic approach to government and political matters. The more we lament our lack of political power, the more reason we have to be uninvolved in the political process. At the core of the most pressing problems facing our nation are political decisions that must be made by people, not just by the President of our country. These decisions cannot be made in the domain of daydreams or on the battlegrounds of bull sessions. They must be decided in the arena of everyday life by ordinary people like you and me.

Considering the emphasis laid on citizenship in the Bible, I was particularly pleased by the resolution on social

86

action adopted by our church body at its Denver convention in 1969. That resolution stated in part:

> But he [the Christian] is also to participate in its [the world's] government and economics and in every aspect of secular society, employing all the resources of judgment and common sense, in order that even this fallen world may experience, as a gift of divine mercy, the greatest possible measure of secular freedom, dignity, justice, peace, and joy. (*Convention Proceedings,* Resolution 9-09)

This statement recognizes that God loves His world and wants to bless it through the lives of Christians.

There are many significant differences between the world of the 1970s and the world of the 1470s. Not the least of these differences is that today life is inexorably bound to political systems. The major problems that face our world and our country can be solved only through political action. Such things as poverty, pollution, racism, peace, prosperity, health, education—the list is endless—are all political problems. The needs are so massive, the stakes are so high, the means are so specialized that corporate action among citizens is required for the welfare of humanity.

Five hundred years ago, about the time that Europeans were first discovering North America, the situation in the church and in the world was quite different from today. And it was at that time that the theology of the separation of church and state was developed for some very good reasons. The crown and the clergy were constantly at each other's throats in power plays tagged by historians as "caeseropapism." This struggle worked to the detriment of society. A modus vivendi had to be reached whereby each would let the other live in relative peace by respecting each other's domain of authority and expertise.

Today the divisions within the Holy Roman Empire can be exceeded only by those found within Christianity. When there was an emperor with great political power and a clerical system with great secular and spiritual power, the situation was explosive. But the emperor is gone, and so is the outward structure of a holy universal church. Christians, whose main reason for being sometimes appears to be the construction of church buildings, parking lots, and parsonages, may well continue to be threatened by a government that talks periodically about taxing those stony testimonials to faith. But they are no longer concerned that government leaders will tell them who their pastors should be or what articles of faith they must accept.

Similarly, government leaders may still have their prayer breakfasts and invite clergymen to pray at inauguration festivities. But these are usually little more than superstitious rituals to which clergymen supposedly add dignity. The church no longer invests the political leader with his powers. And so it should be. There is no need for church and state to fear each other any longer.

Nor is it necessary to take the position recommended by the social action manual of one of our districts, which states: "The corporate group can and should lift its voice against injustice, indecency, crime, and other ills, without involving itself in political action or specific legal corrective means." If the draft law of our nation is found to be repressive and discriminatory against our theological position—as we said it was in the Denver convention of our church body—then our Synod should not and in fact did not hesitate to call for the repeal of this legislation. Furthermore, our Synod pledged itself to work for the substitution of a new bill that would respect the theological stance of Lutheranism.

Of course the church cannot write legislation. The writing of legislation is the task of those with professional expertise in that field. But if the church allows itself to be isolated from the domain of political action (as it has in many quarters), then it forfeits its right to be the prophet of God in a world for which Christ died.

Although some are of the opinion that we must limit our witness to preaching about moral and ethical issues, this is not possible. At first glance it sounds fine. But there are no major moral or ethical issues that are not also political. And to point to a cancer in society without saying what one believes God's will is in the matter is to be an unauthentic spokesman for our Lord Jesus Christ.

To my mind, there is one common denominator to the problems of America. Spell it any way you like, you must still pronounce it "politics." This is where the power is: the power to see that mercy and justice prevail. This is where the power is: the power to feed the hungry, to clothe the naked, to heal the sick. This is where the power is: the power to seek peace and to be a blessing to all the nations of the earth.

Christians have a right to have a significant piece of that power more than anyone else because they believe and confess that the governing authorities that exist do so by the permissive will of God (Rom. 13). You know the words of Jesus when He stood before Pontius Pilate, that emissary of the Roman government despised by every full-blooded Jew, who did not know the source of the authority that had been thrust upon him. In amazement he asked, "You will not speak to me? Do You not know I have power to release You and power to crucify You?" Where are the Christians who, on behalf of the causes of the least of Christ's disciples, will stand in the halls of justice today and say to the prosecutors, as He did: "You would have no power over Me unless it had been given you from above." (John 19:11)

I suppose I should admit to you that I would like to play at Lent. Wouldn't it be nice to imagine that Christ was the Victim of an unjust social order and an envious religious society and lament Him as a dead hero who advocated loving our neighbors as we love ourselves? Christianity would be so much more comfortable — if it were not for Easter. Lent would then be our excuse to say, "You see, it was always thus, and it will always be thus. The good always lose out. They never have the power. We are the good."

But Good Friday wasn't the end. There was a day when Christ stood before His followers and proclaimed: "*All power* in heaven and on earth has been given to Me. Go therefore and make disciples of all nations" (Matt. 28:18 to 19). Ah, there's the rub. We have the power! If only He hadn't said it! But He promised: "You shall receive power when the Holy Spirit has come upon you; and you shall be My witnesses . . . to the end of the earth" (Acts 1:8). If only He hadn't done it! But it is too late. He is risen! He has poured out the Spirit upon those who are His authentic disciples. And now there is no alternative to using the power He has given to His people. Either we use it or we lose it — not just the power but the name "people of God" too.

Don't be naive, friends. You've heard the old slogan: "You can't legislate morality." You say you've used it a few times? So have I. But it isn't true. The legislative process is one of the most effective moral agents God has instituted. You've read the Bible passages quoted to show that segregation isn't God's will. We had them a long time before we had the desegregation laws. Christian slave-holders had Bibles. Christian apartment-house owners went to church long before they practiced open housing. Many Christians lived in luxury and ease before they became concerned about those destined to live in poverty and in slums. Preachers are usually more concerned about their crabgrass than they are about preserving our land for generations to come. The government is God's. It is as viable a force as there is to accomplish many of His purposes.

We answer to the name of Christian because we believe that Jesus Christ, the Lord of history, died and rose again for the salvation of the whole world. We believe with Paul that God was in Christ, reconciling the world unto Himself. He paid the price for all of our sins. He gives us salvation as a free gift. But with this gift He gives us responsibility for the *ministry* of reconciliation. (2 Cor. 5)

One day Christ fed five thousand with a few loaves and a few fish. He did it because they were hungry. He did it because God cares. That was a great miracle. Then came Easter and the ascension. He's gone; yet He promised that His body would still be here and that it would do greater things than He had done. We are the body of Christ. We can do it, friends. He's given us the power. We can feed five million and witness to five billion — *if* we're willing to be lifted up at the crossroads, that is.

Text:

For there is no authority except from God, and those that exist have been instituted by God. (Rom. 13:1)

Dear Father,
> we acknowledge You as a God whose kingdom is not of this world
>> and as a God whose will is to be done on earth as it is in heaven.

Forgive us for using laws to our own welfare and for becoming empire builders as if that were Your will for us.
Empower us to work for reform of all inadequate laws of Your land
> that a life more pleasing to You
> may evolve in our world.

It is an easy matter to avoid the tensions of implementing change.
Sometimes we are made to appear unclean when we engage in the political process.
We may even be accused of the ultimate heresy: of not being a friend of Caesar.

Preserve us from debilitating fear and from calloused indifference.
Make us bold to put our lives on the cross so that Your will may be done on earth as it is in heaven
> and so that people everywhere will know that You are still a God of power and concern.

Hear our prayer for Jesus' sake. Amen.

Crossroads: Poverty

Dear Father, You made Your Son poor so that we might be rich on account of Him. Help us to understand that miracle and to respond to it. Hear us for Jesus' sake. Amen.

I never cease to be amazed at the way the Scriptures demonstrate themselves to be relevant in age after age. Imagine yourself back in the time of the prophet Amos, about 760 B. C. Israel had reached the height of her territorial expansion. Her military power and her economic affluence would never again be as great as they were at that time. Because of their prosperity, many Israelites were confident that the Lord was showing special favor toward them. This resulted in faithful patronage of the national shrines erected to God. Humanly speaking, I doubt that you could find a more parallel picture than that between Israel of the 760s B. C. and that of the United States of America in the 1970s.

Onto that stage of Israel's history there stepped a shepherd. It was Amos from the small town of Tekoa, and he declared he had been commissioned by God to preach. His was the unfortunate task of proclaiming harsh words in a smooth season. And for his efforts the people expelled him from the royal sanctuary at Bethel. They put a bumper sticker on his burro that read: "Love Israel—or leave it!"

It is understandable that this country preacher encountered such hostility, for he prophesied the destruction of a nation that took pride in its security. Furthermore, he claimed that one of the major reasons for the promised downfall was that the nation was overlooking its poor. The merchants could not wait for the Sabbath to be over; they wanted to trade and make money every day. They cared little about the quality of the product they hawked; the price was what counted. But as their gross national product rose, their gross national compassion declined. The poor were the stupid people to whom one sold bread for twice what it cost others. They had no rights. It was intolerable that a preacher should claim that on account of the indignities foisted upon the poor the haves were going to become the have-nots. And the part of the prophesied punishment that hurt the most was the claim that the people of God — so the affluent called themselves — would experience a famine of hearing His Word. The nation was headed for exile.

On Sunday, March 1, 1970, I found this headline in the *Wisconsin State Journal:* "Menace to the Nation: 2 Conservatives Learn Poverty Is Intolerable." Datelined Washington, the opening thoughts of James Reston are these:

> The idea is beginning to get around that poverty in America is not merely an expensive nuisance but a menace to the security of the republic — what George Bernard Shaw once called "the worst of dangers, the worst of crimes."
>
> The guess here is that thoughtful conservatives in both parties no longer can live happily with their old assumptions and prejudices. This much poverty and this much wealth in the same country, they seem to be saying, is unfair, indecent, and what is more critical, *danger-*

ous. They are affronted by the untidiness, inefficiency, and corruption of the old welfare system, and want to be fair—but mainly they are scared.

This is probably a good thing. It brings the problem of poverty in America down from the realm of ideology and charity on to the more solid ground of self-interest. [Emphasis added]

And with that last sentence the tables are turned. The prophet has come out of Washington and has routed the preachers from their pulpits and the beneficent believers from their birch benches. Now there is a good reason for doing the will of God—*FEAR!*

There was a day when Christians sold their possessions and goods and distributed them to all, as any had need (Acts 2), because they were filled with the Spirit and because they devoted themselves to the apostles' teaching. There are times when we seem to have a less noble motivation for meeting the needs of mankind: a bad viral epidemic might break out in the ghetto and spread like wildfire throughout our land.

Once a young preacher named Timothy admonished his hearers in accord with Paul's advice: "Be rich in good deeds, liberal and generous, thus laying up for [yourselves] a good foundation for the future, so that [you] may take hold of the life which is life indeed" (1 Tim. 6:18-19). Is it possible that we have discovered a different reason for showing concern for the poor? After all, they are more mobile than they used to be. Though we might make them live on the other end of town, we cannot confine them to it, and if their discontent rises too high, they might come to our neighborhood and start shooting, burning, or looting. Many have discovered that though they do not have to live with the poor, they might have to die with them. This is for them a good reason to take some action.

When Peter, James, and John extended the hand of fellowship to Paul and encouraged him to work among the Gentiles, they made one special point according to Paul's memory of the occasion. He reported it this way: "Only they would have us *remember the poor,* which very thing I was eager to do" (Gal. 2:10). And Paul really did it as you know if you read your New Testament (2 Cor. 8 and 9). Today Paul might be forced to sit in a congregational meeting where he would be lectured by church leaders to be *cautious about showing concern for the poor* lest some "good givers" become offended and withhold their offering envelopes or affiliate with some congregation where they will not be troubled by pastors who still expect their people to hear the Word of God and do it.

Little wonder that Jesus once said it would be easier for a camel to go through the eye of a needle than for a rich man to enter the kingdom of God (Matt. 19:24). The older I become and the longer I am in the ministry, the more I can appreciate what I used to think was a terribly harsh statement. If James was right when he defined religion as the visiting of widows and fatherless children and keeping oneself unstained from the world (James 1:27), then so was Jesus correct when he said: "Blessed are you poor, for yours is the kingdom of God. . . . But woe to you that are rich, for you have received your consolation. Woe to you that are full now, for you shall hunger." (Luke 6:20, 24-25)

In preparation to preach this sermon, I read all I could lay hands on. I read the Scriptures and stood accused by a Christ who demanded of disciples that they sell their possessions and give to the poor in exchange for treasures in heaven (Matt. 19:21). I was humbled by the faith of a newly converted tax collector, who had the courage to give half of all he owned to the poor. (Luke 19:8)

But I also read technical reports on government programs for the poor and was sickened at how little is done in our country on behalf of those caught in the poverty cycle. In comparison to what this nation pledges for war —and I fully appreciate the need for armed forces— Lazarus is still begging for crumbs from the rich man's table.

I read horrendous interviews taken from poverty-engulfed people in Appalachia. Until my stomach turned, I looked at pictures of little children and adults whose ribs could be counted from fifty feet. And when I finished surveying everything from the Scriptures to the scholars, I was at the point of despair because I felt as if it was too late. Even if Christians cared—and it is sometimes difficult to believe that most do—it might be too late. As the saying goes: "Where God builds churches, Satan builds chapels!"

To meet the needs of the poor would call for such a drastic reordering of priorities for most congregations that only few could respond creatively. To take poverty seriously would necessitate such revisions in synodical programs that I am not certain The Lutheran Church—Missouri Synod can respond effectively.

It may be too late for us as a nation. Although almost everyone seems agreed that welfare reform is needed, Congress is unable to decide what to do and how to do it. So we continue to live with a patched-up 1935 public-assistance law. There is no way to reclaim food dumped into the ocean, or dollars paid people not to produce food for nourishment and cotton for clothing. I realize that there are economic factors involved in paying farmers not to plant and grow food: it helps to keep the prices high and the economy stable. Why even talk about the report of the United Nations Commission for Social Development? It is a known fact that zoo keepers take better care of their charges than many Christians do of their poor brothers and sisters. Yet we are members one of the other — in church — in our finite home called earth.

It was over a century ago that George Bernard Shaw wrote:

> Such poverty as we have today in our great cities degrades the poor, and infects with its degradation the whole neighborhood in which they live. And whatever can degrade a neighborhood, can degrade a country and a continent and finally the whole civilized world, which is only a large neighborhood.

Return to Amos with me and hear what he said: "They hate him who reproves in the gate, and they abhor him who speaks the truth. Therefore because you trample upon the poor and take from him exactions of wheat, you have built houses of hewn stone, but you shall not dwell in them; you have planted pleasant vineyards, but you shall not drink their wine. . . . Seek good, and not evil, that you may live; and so the Lord, the God of hosts, will be with you, as you have said. Hate evil, and love good, and establish justice in the gate; it may be that the Lord, the God of hosts, will be gracious to the remnant of Joseph." (Amos 5:10-11, 14-15)

Does the word of Amos apply to us? I think it does. Yet he warned that anyone who spoke the truth in days like ours would be despised (5:13). But he also knew that the possibility of rejection was worth the risk because some would repent and because God would undoubtedly respond to them. In fact, after telling his people how inevitable God's destruction was going to be because of their treatment of the poor and other sins, Amos still pleaded on behalf of his contemporaries and said of God: "The Lord repented concerning this; 'It shall not be,' said the Lord." (7:3)

I wish I had the righteousness of Amos that I might so plead on our behalf with the same results. But I do not have it. I am only a sinner like you. But this I know and this I believe: God does not desire our death or our destruction. If we will repent of our sin, God will be quick to forgive us. He loves us with a love that overlooks our most flagrant refusal to do His will.

How comforting it is to know that there is someone whose righteousness exceeds that of Amos who daily pleads for us. I refer to our Lord Jesus Christ. Through Him we have received every blessing from God, including forgiveness for selfishness. He is God's greatest Gift to us, the incarnate reminder that every good gift we have comes from God and ought to be returned to our Father (James 1:16-18). Our faith in what He has done for us enables us to respond to the needs of others.

And there is something else that must be said of God's goodness. He loves those about whom we have been speaking. He wants to rescue from the prison of poverty every person held in that dungeon. Were you impressed by the action of Jesus toward His mother while He was hanging on the cross? It was completely in keeping with His concerns. Since she would now be without a husband and without a son, who would preserve His mother from the pangs of hunger and from the degradation of poverty? So while

Jesus was lifted up at Calvary, He saw her in need, and He also found a Christian to meet that need in the person of John. After all, this is why He was on the cross — because He cares about all of our needs.

What about you? Do you really care about the poor and the needy? If you do, then it is not too late after all — provided you will allow yourself to be lifted up at the crossroads.

Text:

By this we know love, that He laid down His life for us; and we ought to lay down our lives for the brethren. But if anyone has the world's goods and sees his brother in need, yet closes his heart against him, how does God's love abide in him? Little children, let us not love in word or speech but in deed and in truth. (1 John 3:16-18)

God,
　　　You sent us a Son who,
　　　after giving up the prerogative of deity,
　　　lived in such a way that He sometimes
　　　had no place to lay His head.
We know our Lord authenticated His ministry
　　　by preaching to the poor
　　　　　and by healing those whose lives were
　　　　　impoverished by sickness and disease.
The question we raise is
　　　if we must really live
　　　in the same spirit of compassion
　　　as Your Son did.
Do You actually expect us to be as concerned
　　　for the unfortunate as He was?

100

Must we give of ourselves in the same measure
    as He expected His followers to sacrifice?
We know the answer, Lord!
It is written large on the pages of the Scriptures.
There is a voice within us—we believe You are
    speaking there—that answers our questions
    on this subject.
Yet we are relentless prodigals
    taking all we can get for ourselves
    and hoping for some way to escape
    the responsibility of sonship.
Forgive us, Lord,
    and empower us to take what is Yours
    and share it with those in need.
Fill us with such appreciation for Your
    blessings, God,
    that we will joyfully deny ourselves
    and give to those who have not.
Thank you, Lord,
    for being the good Giver-God that you are.
Let Your goodness be apparent to all the world
    through our lives.
Amen.

Crossroads: Pollution

Lord God, with Your many gifts give us gratitude for the same that we may show appreciation for Your blessings in our use of them, through Jesus Christ, our Lord. Amen.

While I was driving along the mountain roads in Colorado last summer, my eye was suddenly caught by a flash of light. It drew my attention to a tiny shanty on the hillside that appeared to be a prospector's cabin. An old man stood in front of the dilapidated building. The flash of light had been caused by the sun reflecting from the bottom of a can he was tossing out of his doorway. I could hardly believe my eyes when I beheld the sea of cans beneath this hermit's cottage. I have no idea where he got his groceries. But one thing was certain, there was no garbage pickup where he lived.

Ultimately my amazement gave way to more reasoned thought, and I was plagued by the question: What would my front lawn look like if every can, bottle, and other piece of nondecomposable material used by my family were strewn there? Fortunately I don't have to think about that question too long because my garbage is picked up each week. That problem is solved. Or is it?

Of course it isn't. We all know that. All I have actually succeeded in doing is transferring my debris from one spot to another. Today we are finally beginning to realize that irresponsible use and treatment of creation is causing a major ecological problem in society known as *pollution*. One wonders whether or not the apex of God's creation will become the cause of the destruction of all that God created.

A recent authoritative report on our ravaged environment contained the statement: "Nearly unnoticed, the scourge of pollution has already spread so far that a few scientists say only a drastic cure can prevent devastation as thorough as that of nuclear holocaust" (*Newsweek*, Jan. 26, 1970, p. 31). And nowhere in the world are people more guilty of polluting the environment than are we who live in the United States of America.

I shall not bore you with statistics to back up my claims. Let me mention just these few facts. *Every year* Americans junk seven million cars, 100 million tires, 20 million tons of paper, 28 billion bottles and 48 billion cans. We produce almost 50 percent of the world's industrial pollution, discarding some 165 million tons of solid waste and pouring 172 million tons of smoke and fumes into the atmosphere. In addition, almost every fruit, vegetable, or grain we eat has been sprayed, dusted, or gassed by some poison and treated by some chemical fertilizer. We spend 2.8 billion dollars a year just to collect garbage. If you want to visualize what that means bulkwise, it has been deduced that the volume of waste discarded by the residents of California in a single year would make a solid wall 100 feet wide by 30 feet high from Oregon to Mexico.

Every year we are faced with tragic losses in wildlife. The brown pelican is the state bird of Louisiana. Perhaps I should say "was" the state bird of Louisiana because there are only about 600 left in America on an island off the shore of California, and they produced only five chicks in a recent year because the rest of their eggs collapsed from weakened shells contaminated by high concentrations of DDT. Even the *Le Leche* society may be in trouble, because nursing American mothers carry in their breasts milk that contains anywhere from three to ten times more of the pesticide DDT than the federal government allows in dairy milk intended for human consumption.

I could go to considerable length listing the overwhelming evidence of the colossal problems with which we are faced. But this should hardly be necessary in a land where one of our major cities, Los Angeles, forbids its children to exercise almost every other day lest they breathe too deeply of polluted air. Who needs convincing when we know for a fact that the fastest-growing cause of death in the United States is the lung disease emphysema?

I fear that we have been hypocritical about our doctrine of creation. To be sure, we have confessed God as Creator. Much heat has resulted from our arguing over the *method* of creation. But what has become lost in the heat of argument is concern for an attitude of thankfulness to God for creation, an attitude that should evidence itself in appreciative action.

Recently I heard of an incident of glass breaking that was unique. The unusual feature of the event to which I refer is that it was told by a pastor who could remember only one glass having been broken in his home even though twelve years passed between the time of the breaking to which he referred and today. The reason that one incident lived on so strongly in the memory of the pastor was that the glass had been given to him by his widowed mother shortly before her death. Although the set of glasses from which the broken glass came was a wedding gift to the pastor's parents, the set was of relatively little financial value. But to the pastor telling the story it was obvious that they were priceless because of the one who gave them to him. The *source* of the gift made the difference.

Then what of creation? If it is indeed the gift of God, given to mankind as a sacred trust, then how can we continue to pillage and plunder the earth to satisfy our selfish pleasures and desires? Is not our relationship to the Giver indicative of how we use the gift? Can we kill little animals for fancy furs to warm our pride or murder magnificent beasts to decorate our mantels and our masculinity or fill our atmosphere with atomic wastes and still honestly confess, "I believe in God the Father almighty, Maker of heaven and earth"? Is it consistent with our doctrine of creation that we should allow our swamps to be filled with refuse or run the risk of making not only our lakes and rivers uninhabitable to life but also our oceans? Is God Creator *only* of human life, or is He indeed Creator of *all* forms of life? If we do not regret the loss of *His* gifts to us as deeply as we deplore the destruction of some human gift, then our theology of creation is but words at best.

Of course you realize that there is an obvious link between population, productivity, and pollution. To solve our problem, we must limit and reverse our population trend. But what must happen until this can be accomplished? Again men of science are speaking in symphony with Scripture. They are saying that our answer lies *not in technology but in abstinence.*

The body of Jesus Christ raised on Calvary's cross was His eternal no to materialism. You remember how Satan capped the first temptation of a fasting man to turn stones into bread by leading Christ to an exceedingly high mountain from which He might behold all the kingdoms of the world and the glory of them (Matt. 4). These kingdoms were to be Satan's gift to our Lord if only He would give up His redemptive task. It took until Calvary for Christ to give substance to His courageous reply: "Begone, Satan!" Jesus chose another high spot, Golgotha, the place of the skull, from which to show man a better way of life. He forfeited comforts, pleasures, and the prestige of fatherhood in a Jewish community that He might reconcile to God the Father the world and all those in it. That which we so blithely destroy was purchased and dedicated to God at a most precious price.

Abstinence! That is a large part of the answer to our problem. Self-denial is a great part of the solution. There is no need for Christians of the United States of America to exploit the world we live in if we truly find our greatest pleasure in God and His people. It is high time that we begin purchasing and using only what we really need and can efficiently use. And even then we must begin to reuse what we have and be done with our wasteful "throw-away" economy. We must no longer tolerate or encourage by financial support the exploitation of man and nature by selfish interests whose tackle box contains all sorts of bait, ranging from shifting hemlines to luxury travel.

It is ironic that we Christians have made fun of people who idolize rocks and trees and rivers and animals. We call them pagans because they reverence creation. Yet in our enlightened Christianity we commit the greater sin because we worship gods of brick and asphalt and stainless steel and aluminum. Paul says that no coveter, who is an *idolater*, shall enter God's kingdom. Let's be honest about it: as a nation and as individuals we are among the greatest coveters the world has ever known.

It is time to return to Calvary, to take up crosses, and in true discipleship to suffer with Christ. It is time to walk in the way of Jesus and to practice self-denial. Some fasting would be good for all of us. Our fasting could also benefit nature and other people. As Christians we ought to engage in a joyous but responsible use of God's creation, so that our actions confirm our confessions. In being called to have dominion over nature we were commissioned to rule for its welfare not its destruction.

We have made a garbage dump out of God's beautiful garden. But we also made killers out of wonderful creatures created in the image of God. God is accumstomed to our acts of rebellion and their terrible consequences. There could be nothing more atrocious than the death of His sinless Son because of our greed and lust for power. Yet, would you believe it — *He loves us nevertheless!* He really does.

God loves us all despite the ungrateful way we have treated Him and His wonderful works. God forgives us for our rebellion. He loves us so much that He will strengthen us when we are ready to make the sacrifices called for by this crisis. There is cause for hope — if we act immediately and decisively. If we can get our government to give as serious attention to this problem as it has given to flying to the moon and to Mars, I believe we can survive. There is hope if each one of us and ours is willing to be lifted up at the crossroads. There is hope because Jesus Christ mounted a cross for us that through His death and rising again He might be Lord of history — God's Son through whom everything has purpose and meaning. God give you courage!

Text:

"All things are lawful," but not all things are helpful. "All things are lawful," but not all things build up. Let no one seek his own good but the good of his neighbor. (1 Cor. 10: 23-24)

Crossroads: Peace

Lord God, You sent Your Son to bring peace on earth.
Bring it in our time for the sake of the suffering of
Jesus Christ. Amen.

A cartoon in the March 22, 1969, issue of the *Saturday Review* poked fun at the Scriptural admonition to beat swords into plowshares. Taking the prophet's admonition literalistically, the cartoon depicted a character dressed like one of the three musketeers standing with sword in hand before a perspiring blacksmith. With an agonized expression the smith asked, "How big a plowshare did you have in mind?"

In my lifetime I do not know when there has been a greater longing for peace in our world than there is today. Recent polls indicate that the majority of American citizens are becoming intolerant of the efficiently run business of war—a business honed sharp by science so that men can destroy and kill with the refinement and skill of the laboratory experiment.

How do you think God would judge us as a people considering these brief facts? We are the only nation of the world to drop an atomic bomb on another land that shares our globe. Years of time and countless dollars of taxpayers' money have been spent to develop poisonous gas, nauseous gas, and deadly germs for biological warfare, some of which we are now attempting to destroy "safely" in our oceans. The United States is one of the few major nations of the world that still have not signed the anti-genocide treaty of the United Nations. Recently we appear to be concerned about the welfare of our enemies when they are destroyed personally and inefficiently as at My Lai. A team of American scientists reported at the end of 1970 that the United States destroyed by plant-killing chemicals $500,000,000 worth of timber and enough rice to feed 600,000 persons for a year and damaged the health of human beings, especially the unborn babies of South Vietnam (cf. *National Observer,* January 4, 1971, p. 11). When we behold ourselves in a looking glass, it is hard for a sensible Christian to escape the conclusion that God's will for us must be that we strive more earnestly to achieve *peace* in our world.

But come on a flashback with me. Consider the important role that the subject of peace plays in the Holy Scriptures. There are only a few unifying themes that tie both Old and New Testaments together. One that does is *peace.*

As used in the Old Testament, the basic word for peace, *shalom,* means having all relationships in harmony. It is a very comprehensive term covering all of the activities of life. It refers to the well-being and wholesomeness that should be a normal part of man's relationship with his fellowman, especially with those to whom one is most closely related. To preserve the family peace, you recall, Abram said to Lot: "Let there be no strife between you and me and between your herdsmen and my herdsmen; for we are kinsmen. . . . Separate yourself from me. If you take the left hand, then I will go to the right; or if you take the right hand, then I will go to the left." (Gen. 13:8-9)

After Gideon had been visited by an angel, he built an

110

altar to the Lord and called it "The Lord is peace" (Judges 6:24). God is often referred to as the God of peace in the New Testament as well (Rom. 5:33; 16:20; 1 Cor. 14:33). Although there was considerable violence and warfare throughout the history of the people of Old Testament times, the prophets usually interpreted the necessity for killing and being killed as a result of man's sin and rebellion against God. Peace was closely associated with righteousness on the part of God's people. Political and social turmoil were considered to be results of God's punitive judgment, geared to bring Israel to repentance and reformation.

At the height of Israel's frustration with prolonged conflict, there developed a desire for an opportunity to escape war. This longing worked itself out in the expression of an eschatological hope that promised a paradisal existence for the faithful where there would be no war or strife. (Is. 2:1-4)

It is interesting to note that the New Testament authors, especially Luke, marked the beginning of this "promised time" with the births of John the Baptist and of Jesus Christ. For instance, in Luke's song of Zechariah are the words: "And you, child, will be called the prophet of the Most High; for you will go before the Lord to prepare His ways . . . to guide our feet into the way of *peace*" (Luke 1:76, 79). We are most familiar with the words attributed by Luke to the angel who announced Christ's birth to the shepherds: "Glory to God in the highest and on earth *peace*, goodwill among men." (Luke 2:14)

Jesus pointed out that those who work for peace reflect the image of God. In His mountain sermon he said: "Blessed are the peacemakers, for they shall be called sons of God" (Matt. 5:9). Christ was not only a peacemaker, but

He was also a peace-giver. To the woman whom He healed from the issue of blood He said, "Daughter, your faith has made you well; go in peace" (Luke 8:48). And to His followers He gave the coveted gift with these words: "Peace I leave with you; My peace I give to you." (John 14:27)

The crucifixion and resurrection of Jesus have much to do with our peace. He assured the disciples that in the midst of the world's tribulation they could still have peace because He overcame the world (John 16:33). And to frightened followers His usual postresurrection greeting was: "Peace be with you" (John 20:19, 26). The disciples understood this greeting as more than a shallow "Hello." Jesus gave His followers peace. Paul affirmed that all creation was empowered for peace with God and with man, that Christ made peace for all by the blood of His cross. (Col. 1:19-20)

There is power in the peace God gives. Christ's peace is a *ruling* peace that determines our actions and controls our behavior (Col. 3:15). There is something so magnificent about it that it defies all understanding (Phil. 4:7). It can empower us to love even our natural enemies (Eph. 2:14-18). God communicates the gift of peace to us by the Holy Spirit. (Gal. 5:22)

And do we need it? Oh, how we do! It is too true what Christ said: that out of our hearts come evil thoughts, including murder and other desires that defile a man (Matt. 15:19). Also James was on target when he wrote: "What causes wars, and what causes fightings among you? Is it not your passions that are at war in your members? You desire and do not have; so you kill. And you covet and cannot obtain; so you fight and wage war. . . . Cleanse your hands, you sinners, and purify your hearts, you men of

112

double mind. . . . Humble yourselves before the Lord, and He will exalt you" (James 4:1-2, 8, 10). Thus we have come full circle from Abram to the ABM. What James wrote is as true today as it ever was, and until we take his message seriously, we shall not know peace, not even with the finest antiballistic missile system our tax dollars can buy.

Who knows to what extent *greed* is responsible for hostility between our nation and other nations of the world? Who knows how *double-minded* we may have been in befriending countries whose natural resources we could exploit for our own purposes? With the standard of living we enjoy in these United States, we need troops on foreign shores.

It is time that we as individual Christians and as citizens of the United States of America begin to give serious attention to reordering our priorities. Can we honestly seek peace and at the same time spend as much money for war as we have in recent years? Should it not be clear to us that the more we arm ourselves to the teeth the more *insecure* we are? How pathetic it was to hear the closing words of Secretary McNamara when he made his famous ABM announcement in 1967! Said McNamara: "In the end, the root of man's security does not lie in his weaponry."

We live in a *democracy,* Christian friends. Hence the responsibility for such decisions rests squarely on the shoulders of each one of us. We are also responsible for the actions of our nation as Msgr. Marvin Bordelon, director of the Division of World Justice and Peace, U. S. Catholic Conference, recently stated:

> In other words, are the soldiers who did the killing at
> My Lai almost two years ago any more guilty than the

113

B52 crews who continue to this very day to systematically destroy villages in the so-called 'free-fire' zones? Are they more guilty than those who order such actions? Or than the people of the United States who are ultimately responsible for public policy? (*The National Register,* Dec. 21, 1969)

I don't like to think of myself as being responsible for a massacre, and I don't imagine you relish the thought either. Well, if you don't, then you should be certain that you are doing all you can to bring God's will of peace on earth to fruition. As God's servants there is much you can do to accomplish His will.

Think peace and do peace! That is the message to you. Our Lord Jesus Christ allowed His body to be raised to the sky in suffering and death that we might dwell peaceably with God and with one another. His sacrifice dramatically demonstrates that the prize of peace is not won easily. True peace happens only where there are people of goodwill, human beings who consciously limit their own desires, who are prepared to forgive and to minister to their enemies, who are ready to turn the other cheek because they are committed to the principle that good cannot come out of evil that is compounded.

There is hope for peace in our day because God wills it. There is hope for peace now because God is raising up bold, new prophets to proclaim it and to work toward achieving it. There is hope for peace in our lifetime because God will forgive us for our selfishness and aggression. And this forgiveness will move us to repentance and to more responsible use of His blessings. There is hope for peace soon because the love God has shown in sending a Son into our world to die for it will motivate many of us to gather at the crossroads of our nation where we too may be lifted up by God as a sign of peace to our world.

Text:

Repay no one evil for evil, but take thought for what is noble in the sight of all. If possible, so far as it depends upon you, live peaceably with all. Beloved, never avenge yourselves, but leave it to the wrath of God; for it is written, "Vengeance is Mine, I will repay, says the Lord." No, "if your enemy is hungry, feed him; if he is thirsty, give him drink. . . ." Do not be overcome by evil, but overcome evil with good. (Rom. 12:17-21)

> O Lord of Hosts,
> You have bedeviled us,
>   and Satan's leash seems longer
>   than it used to be.
> You have taken
>   all the dash and gallantry
>   out of war.
> There are no longer
>   any wars to read about,
>   wars to discuss.
>
> We are all sitting
>   in one another's laps,
>   and there is blood
>   on all our hands.
> Every shot fired anywhere
>   is aimed at all of us:
>   a shot fired in Biafra
>   nicks the Washington Monument

and richochets
round Trafalgar Square.

We are hard put to find
a cleanly righteous cause.
We are always fighting wars
we know no one will ever win,
wars it does not pay to fight.
And millions watch their butter—
if they know what butter is—
go up in acrid smoke
or plummet earthward
in a packaged hell.

*All who take the sword
will perish by the sword.*
We know now,
sobered by Your medicine:
Your Son, our Lord, spoke truth;
wars are the key signature
of our perishing world.
And we must wait
and hope
and pray,
" *Thy* kingdom come!"

(Martin H. Franzmann, *Pray for Joy*
[St. Louis: Concordia Publishing House, 1970],
pp. 14-15)

Crossroads: Oneness

Dear God, in little more than thirty years Your Son walked the distance from Bethlehem to Calvary that we who call You "Our Father" might be one. Make us willing to walk as far to demonstrate our oneness to Your world. Hear us for Jesus' sake. Amen.

Our fathers had a dream! It was a vision in which the dreamers saw a land settled and occupied by people with common goals, common hopes, and a common destiny. The fathers named their dream. They called it The United States of America.

The dream was more easily named than implemented. Not long after a common enemy had been defeated, it became apparent that there were great differences in the philosophies of those who wanted to give direction to this new nation, and it was less than 100 years old when a war had been fought in which it was not uncommon to have members of the same family fighting against each other. Another 100 years have passed since the Civil War, and it is apparent that there are still divisions among us that evidence themselves in hateful action.

In the South are roving bands of whites armed with axe handles beating blacks and overturning school buses. In Madison, Wisconsin, we have old men who spit at Palm Sunday peace marchers and young men and women who break plate-glass windows and shout obscenities at police. In the East and West there are bombers and burners. Postal workers defy the highest authority of the land, and farmers threaten to burn the barns of those who take their potatoes to market. From cities to rural areas there is turmoil, and it becomes increasingly more difficult to say, "I pledge allegiance to the United States of America" because the idea of a *United* States is fast becoming a myth.

But I suppose we should not be too surprised that things are so hectic in our world. After all, even the church, the body of Christ, has had its moments in history when Christians killed and persecuted fellow Christians with a vengeance and refinement of cruelty of which one would imagine only the vilest person on earth to be capable. And such behavior is so far from the will of God that one would think it to be impossible.

God wants His people to be one. He despises all evidence of their disunity. The Epistle lesson traditionally used by the Christian church on Maundy Thursday is taken from First Corinthians. Within that book alone are more references to the evils of factionalism than I would care to mention in one brief sermon. Consider these words from First Corinthians One:

"I appeal to you, brethren, by the name of our Lord Jesus Christ, that all of you agree and that there be no dissensions among you, but that you be united in the same mind and the same judgment."

Paul's deep concern over the dissension of Christians is evidenced in many places throughout the letter, as in the third chapter, where he wrote: "For while there is jealousy and strife among you, are you not of the flesh and behaving like ordinary men?" It is with concern for unity that Paul introduced his version of the institution of our Lord's Supper:

118

"But in the following instructions I do not commend you, because when you come together, it is not for the better but for the worse. For in the first place, when you assemble as a church, I hear that there are divisions among you." (1 Cor. 11:17-18)

For the welfare of our world, the church, and even our beloved Missouri Synod, it is time that we began to take seriously God's will for our unity. Someone has got to take the initiative. Someone must show people a better way. There is no reason why that someone should not be ourselves.

After all, we are heirs to God's will that we lead a life worthy of our calling. And according to Paul's Letter to the Ephesians, this means being eager to maintain the unity of the Spirit in the bond of peace (Eph. 4:1-6). In Romans 12 you can find the call to Christians that they live in harmony with one another and associate with the lowly. In Second Corinthians 13 you will hear Paul admonishing Christians to mend their ways and agree with one another. Paul implied in his Letter to the Ephesians that the only thing he yet desired of those believers was that they learn to be of the same mind. Likewise Peter admonished his readers to have unity of spirit, sympathy, and love for one another. (1 Peter 3:8)

Surely I do not have to allude to more Bible passages. There can be no doubt about God's will in this matter. Few points are as clearly made in the Scriptures as that God wants His people to live in peace and harmony with one another. Our Savior Himself said on the night that we commemorate each Maundy Thursday:

"I do not pray for these only but also for those who believe in Me through their word, that they may all be one . . .

so that the world may believe that Thou hast sent Me. The glory which Thou hast given Me I have given to them that they may be one even as We are one . . . that they may become perfectly one, so that the world may know that Thou hast sent Me and hast loved them even as Thou hast loved Me." (John 17:20-23)

Since we recognize God's will in this matter, it remains only for us to discover how we can do it. Here God Himself comes to our rescue. He pours out His *one* Spirit upon us; He calls us through the Spirit into His *one* body, the Christian church; He initiates us through *one* Baptism into living relationship with our *one* Lord; and He is willing to be the *one* Father of us all. (Eph. 4:1-6)

The first direction that oneness must travel is upward. The vertical relationship of unity must be established before there is hope for any real and lasting oneness among ourselves. That this very thing may happen, Christ gives us His body, His blood, and His power as well. (1 Cor. 10; John 17)

To be sure, there are times when we strain at the binding cords of God's love like marionettes who might think they could run and dance without their strings. But as we crumple in a helpless heap, the puppeteer of heaven scoops us up and restores us to a useful life on His stage. And we are ashamed and embarrassed at our stupidity, but He understands. He loves us.

When we are confident of His love and control in our lives, we are also free to reach out to other players around us, knowing that He cares as much for them as He does for us. It is then that we find joy in the presence of other pilgrims and become motivated to confirm our vertical relationship by entering into horizontal bonds.

The cords that bind us to one another are as much the work of God as the strings that tie us to His mercy and love. A common faith, a common Baptism, a common Savior, a common Spirit, a common loaf, and a common cup—these are the strands out of which comes unity. When the vertical bonds are strong enough, they enable us to extend the hand of fellowship to the most despicable of God's people that they may not be lost to the fold. Being aware of our own unworthiness and rejoicing that God freely chose us to be among His people, no one will be distasteful to us.

One of the crossroads that must be faced in our day is that of unity. The world should be able to look to the church for guidance and direction in this important matter. I believe that it can if there are enough of us who are willing to go to the crossroads and to be lifted up in self-sacrifice for a sign of oneness.

America stands at the crossroads—as a nation—as a significant part of the people of God. What happened at Calvary makes a difference. The crucifixion of Jesus Christ affects all of life. Because of Christ's sacrifice, there are still those who are prepared to take up their crosses and follow after Him. Out of that minority God will work unity and save His people.

Text:
I speak as to sensible men; judge for yourselves what I say. The cup of blessing which we bless, is it not a participation in the blood of Christ? The bread which we break, is it not a participation in the body of Christ? Because there is one bread, we who are many are one body, for we all partake of the one bread. (1 Cor. 10:15-17)

Lord,

    let us not partake of the body and blood of our Savior
without discerning that we are His body, the church.

Give us the courage to celebrate our oneness.

    Make us willing to sacrifice as much for it as Christ did
or as the leaders of our country did to preserve its
unity.

We praise you that in this Maundy Thursday meal we sense
our unity with believers who have rested from their
labors long ago.

Save us from the hypocrisy of celebrating that oneness
while preserving unnecessary separations among the
saints who live today.

You have made us one!

    Through Christ You have brought us into the unity
of Father, Son, and Spirit.

    Preserve us in that relationship for the sake of Him who
shed body and blood for us.

Amen!

Crossroads: Death

Lord God, in the midst of death we are in life. Help us to remember this truth and live it. Amen.

At regular intervals journalists wishing to sell articles write about the crisis of death. Recently this story was given a new twist by a writer who spoke of the crisis of mourning among Americans. The author suggested that the technological age we live in robs us of the privacy we need to air our grief about death. The attitude of the article was reminiscent of the pre-Christian view toward dying.

It is true that the mass-media manner in which we are exposed to death tends to make us calloused toward it. Radio, television, and newspaper bring us daily and weekly totals of enemy and ally deaths from various battlefields around our world. The highway death toll is kept on the street corner of the busiest intersections of towns and cities on billboards not dissimilar from a number system used to wait on customers at the meat market. Through the miracle of satellite television our living room becomes the battlefield, and we can watch bombs drop and bodies explode while drinking beer and eating popcorn. It takes a family experience with death to move most of us sympathetically. Statistics concerning how many children die from starvation each day are wholly inadequate to arouse our sincere concern.

But what should be our attitude toward death at a time when one of the world's major problems is overpopulation?

Many are seriously raising the question about how long the medical profession should be allowed to use heroic methods to sustain life temporarily at great expense to families and society. Scientists are looking to the church for answers to these perplexing questions. Many are willing to discuss such issues with clergymen. Frankly, I cannot conceive of treating the subject of death apart from the one that occurred on Calvary's hilltop when one Man surrendered His life for all of us.

To my mind, death is one of the topics that most clearly demonstrate the difference between the Old Covenant and the New Covenant. According to Old Testament literature death marks man as being radically different from God. God revealed Himself to Moses as the One who always was and is and will be. The Old Covenant man lived with the awareness that a time would come when he would be no more (Ps. 39:13). Death was catastrophic. To die was to be cut off from the land of the living, to be separated from the presence of God, to be disconnected from the memory of God, to be unable to praise God. (Ps. 6:5; 30:9; 88:10-12; 115:17; Is. 38:18)

Armed with a radical apocalyptic theology (Is. 25:8; Dan. 12:2), Christ walked into the gloom and doom of an old relationship between God and His people and dispelled the dreariness of death with a Gospel of life. It was too much for faithful Sadducees to accept (Mark 12:18-27). It seemed too unbelievable to be true. But true it was, or the sword that struck at Malchus might not have been restrained. If it was not so, the sin of Adam might have killed us all—dead! (Rom. 5:12-21; 1 Cor. 15:20-26)

The dilemma of death was more than neutralized when Christ allowed His body to be raised on a cross for us. The

124

writer of Hebrews put it this way: "Since therefore the children share in flesh and blood, He Himself likewise partook of the same nature that through death He might destroy him who has the power of death, that is, the devil, and deliver all those who through fear of death were subject to lifelong bondage" (Heb. 2:14-15). Because of Calvary, death is but a sleep for the faithful (1 Thess. 4:13-18). Those united to Christ in baptism have died already (Rom. 6:3, Col. 2:12). Paul claimed that after Good Friday to live was Christ and to die was gain. (Phil. 1:21)

At a time when the emphasis of the covenant relationship between God and His people was primarily on a kingdom of this world, death made little sense. Death meant defeat. There was good reason for the dejection of disciples who had not grasped until after the ascension that the new kingdom was not of this world. A Christ of Calvary in terms of the Old Covenant meant little more than that God's people had experienced another glimpse of glory only to see it fade and fail like a comet streaking across the sky.

But a new era was ushered in one Friday afternoon, when the sun failed and the curtain of the temple was torn in two. It was the hour of Christ's death, and from the moment when He cried, "Father, into Thy hands I commit My spirit!" (Luke 23:46) dying for those who believed in Him would never be the same. The death of Christ, validated by His resurrection, secured the forgiveness of our sins and demonstrated that the way to transform the world was by complete self-giving in total sacrifice to a loving Father-God. Having caught that vision, many of the greatest leaders of our nation, both black and white, have offered it more in their death than those who have jealously guarded their lives.

Of course there is a place for grief when friends and loved ones die. We will miss their warm and lively presence as we would if they were to take an extended vacation someplace where we would not be with them. That is sad. We get lonely for loved ones. We should not fear to vent our feelings at such times of separation, but neither should we grieve as those who have no hope. For as Paul says, it is the Christ Crucified who is Christ the Power of God and the Wisdom of God (1 Cor. 1:23-24). The Word of the cross is the power of God. (1 Cor. 1:18)

Concerning the death with which we are daily surrounded, we must avoid the twin perils of hopeless grief and of pagan indifference. It matters how many children die of starvation and how many people die on our nation's highways and how many more are slaughtered on the battlefields of the world. Life is God's gift which we are to sustain and nurture. Death is intended to be useful and purposeful if Good Friday has any meaning. It is not to be dreaded as in Old Covenant times. Nor is it to be treated indifferently as it often appears to be in our time.

When life-and-death decisions must be made, the question that should help to clarify action is, what would be most helpful in this case? (Phil. 1:19-26.) How would God's will be served most completely? It should be obvious that when such questions are asked we approach our Calvary long before we are about to expire. The hour of our death, be it known or unknown to ourselves, is but the culmination of the life we planned to live and give to God. Through such determination we take up our cross and follow Jesus. Giving ourselves completely to a loving heavenly Father, we will be surprised by crucifixion no more than Christ was.

But even when we spend a lifetime preparing ourselves for death, there are times when we waver and weaken. Perhaps it was this human trait that cried so loudly from the cross: "My God, My God, why have You forsaken Me?" Remember those words during your fretful moments. A Man went through it all for you, experiencing one of the cruelest methods of death known to mankind. But wrestling with the impostor, death, did not weaken Him beyond the point of confidence in a loving Father God, and it will not drive you beyond that point either.

God loves you. He forgives your sins. He is with you now and at the hour of your death. You have already died with Christ in your baptism. You were baptized into His death (Rom. 6). Because He willingly died on Calvary and rose again, your life of self-giving has great meaning in the kingdom of God. The sting and victory of death have been taken away. Having sung a song of mockery into the face of death, Paul wrote: "Therefore, my beloved brethren, be steadfast, immovable, always abounding in the work of the Lord, knowing that in the Lord your labor is not in vain." (1 Cor. 15:58)

Because of Christ, your life will not be lived for nothing, nor will your death be for naught. He died for you and for me. We give up our lives for Him as the Spirit guides us. We welcome the Crossroads!

Text:

It was now about the sixth hour, and there was darkness over the whole land until the ninth hour, while the sun's light failed; and the curtain of the temple was torn in two. Then Jesus, crying with a loud voice, said, "Father, into Thy hands I commit My spirit!" And having said this, He breathed His last. (Luke 23:44-46)

Lord,
    we are born to die in service to You.
Help us so to use our lives
    that we do not fear our calvaries
    nor hopelessly mourn those who are raised on their
        crosses before our turn arrives.
Give us opportunities
    to use our lives as sacrificially as Your Son invested
        His life in Your service.
Thank you
    for His life,
    His death,
    His rising again.
    Amen.

Crossroads: Life

Lord, by Your mercy free us to celebrate the life we have
received from You on account of our Lord's resurrection.
In His name we speak our prayer. Amen.

Only on rare occasions does one discover a fresh
statement of the meaning of the great festivals we celebrate
in the Christian church. I recently came upon an Easter
affirmation that impressed me as a meaningful contemporary
witness to the empty tomb. It was written by Jaroslav Vajda
and entitled "Oh, to Be Reborn!"

> Oh, to be reborn!
> > to be able to return to the womb
> > > and begin again;
> > this time to choose one's parents,
> > > one's color, one's birthplace,
> > > one's family, one's future;
> > to start with a clean slate,
> > > avoid the stupid mistakes,
> > > grasp the missed opportunities,
> > > capture the moment;
> > this time to be wise,
> > > understanding, loving,
> > > and to value each gift of love;
> > this time to live fully,
> > > every minute of the brief span.

Foolish dream!

The womb is closed,
   the leopard's spots do not change,
   we bind ourselves with the ropes
      of past errors and failures,
   we limp along on legs long crippled.

But a Man rises from the dead —
   as He promised He would —
and comes forth with a new body,
   a whole new life;
and He grips my putrefying body
   with His vigorous hands,
lifts me to my feet,
peers into my eyes, and says:
   "Because I live,
      you will live also!"

Oh, for the moment of rebirth!
   Oh, for the break of that day!

But look! It hasn't yet arrived,
   and I feel my heart beating
      with a new pulse,
   my blood throbs with a happy surge,
   I am already somebody new:
      I think new, I feel new, I see new,
      I react new, I love new, I live new.

He said: "I am the Resurrection
      and the Life,"
   and I said: "You really are!"
   And it is as if I were born again!

What a taste, what a coaxing,
   insatiable taste

of what is still to come
in all its fullness!

To be reborn! And I am! And I will be!
(*This Day,* March 1967)

One of the most exciting things about the age we live in is that ours is a time of rediscovery. It is happening all about us in almost every field of human endeavor. For instance, the scientific world is helping us to realize once again that we human beings are part of a living system, dependent on and related to every other form of life that exists on our planet. That restatement of an old truth is good news, and we wonder how it could have been overlooked for so long a time.

The church can add its voice to such a reemphasis this Easter season and proclaim yet another truth. Broadcasting the message of the ancient Book of Deuteronomy (8:3b), we must stress that man is capable of life more profound and more complete than physical existence. As Christians we affirm completely that man shares life with other species, but we confess as well faith in a life that cannot be sustained by bread alone but is dependent on the self-disclosure of God through His Son Jesus Christ. We wonder and stand in awe before the diversity of biological life with which we are surrounded. But we find our greatest potential to utilize the life we have in the nourishment we receive from the Bread of Life, even our risen Savior. As Christians we believe it is what *He* has done for us that enables us to move from humanity to personhood.

John, the gospel writer, has the knack for saying profound things very simply. He made the point I am attempting to communicate to you this way: Of the Christ he said, "In Him was life, and the life was the light of men" (John 1:4). John maintained that those who were in Christ had a special kind of life not found among those who were not in relationship to their Lord. Jesus called it *eternal* life. And just as He taught that living people could be dead, so He also proclaimed that eternal life could be the possession of believers who were very much living in this world. John recorded Christ's comment on the subject this way: "Truly, truly, I say to you, he who hears My Word and believes Him who sent Me, has eternal life; he does not come into judgment but has passed from death to life." (John 5:24)

It was for life that Jesus became a human being. Recall His statement: "The thief comes only to steal and kill and destroy; I came that they may have life and have it abundantly" (John 10:10). He who proclaimed Himself to be the Living Water and the Bread of Life said: "As the living Father sent Me and I live because of the Father, so he who eats Me will live because of Me" (John 6:57). Because Jesus Christ is Life and came that we might have life in His name (John 20:31), He was able to lay down His life in service to all mankind. When He was consumed by people, He had power to take up His life again to reign and to call us to follow His example. The meaning of Easter is truly glorious as He captures it in His words: "Truly, truly, I say to you, unless a grain of wheat falls into the earth and dies, it remains alone; but if it dies, it bears much fruit. He who loves his life loses it, and he who hates his life in this world will keep it for eternal life." (John 12:24-25)

There are two ways to live life. One is characterized by these famous words from Shakespeare's *Macbeth:*

[Life] is a tale
Told by an idiot, full of sound and fury,
Signifying nothing.

(Act 5, sc. 5, lines 26-28)

To have that philosophy of life is to be caught up in mere existence. It is to be driven by passion to kill the king for one's own gain but to be paralyzed by fear and hence incapable of satisfying desire. It is to be bold enough to plunge a dagger into a sleeping monarch but unable to wash away the guilt of greed's actions. It is to be dead while living.

There are many dead people walking around in our world without their tombstones. You can recognize them by their insecurities. They aren't sure of their life at all. They cling to it jealously, never having time for the needs or joys of others. They are overcautious, rarely willing to take a risk for another human being. They are the "I don't want to get involved" crowd. They are the "I don't have time for that" people. They are the ones who have financial resources only for their own desires despite the fact that they enjoy a standard of living far superior to those who would profit from their generosity.

Such corpses are not strangers to church buildings. They often park in church pews and sport pious poses that are becoming to their true condition. Like those who whistle in graveyards, they usually speak their lifeless lines quite loudly at voters' meetings. Such lifeless, so-called Christians can usually be recognized as those who always want to play it safe and to go along with the crowd instead of taking the risk of being one of the Twelve and sticking with Him who has the words of eternal life. (John 6:68)

Fortunately, there is another way to live life. It is characterized by the Christ, who said: "For this reason the Father loves Me, because I lay down My life that I may take it again. No one takes it from Me, but I lay it down of My own accord. I have power to lay it down, and I have power to take it again" (John 10:17-18). This is the lifestyle to which we who are called by His name are summoned. And praise God! there are many living in our times who truly are alive.

Just like the dead ones, such lively people may be found in all stations and situations of life. Some are among the young people of our society who selflessly search for truth and the things that make for peace. Some are in the ring of politics, where they are willing to take a blow on the chin that liberty and justice might prevail. Some are in the church, courageously enduring the wrath of dead people by ministering to lively saints who need encouragement and opportunity to put their lives on the line for Christ in meeting the needs of the least of His people. And would you believe it? Others hardly ever grace church buildings because they find the formality of the institutional church too confining to their life style. But they are all in Christ. He is the Life of all the living!

It is only the Lord of life who could give us the command to hang loosely onto all that is ordinarily connected with life in this world. He did it! That is His credential for demanding it of each of us. But not only does He demand that we really live; He enables us to really live. He gives us the abundant life. He is the Bread and Water of Life for us. He is the Light of our life. These are all symbols that proclaim Christ to be the sustaining force of life in God's kingdom.

One of the great blessings of the Easter miracle is the promise of resurrection for us. Because of Easter I can say to those of you who are still dead in trespasses and sins: Come alive! Join the Easter generation. It's not too late. You can rise from the dead with Christ *right now*. You can do it today if you want to. Your faith and baptism make it possible (John 6; Rom. 6). Believe on the Lord Jesus Christ. He is the eternal Word of the living God. He is not dead but alive, and because He lives, *you* shall live also. Have life! It's here for you.

And to those of you who are already alive because of Christ I say, "Good for you! Keep on living. Don't fear dying." Jesus said: "I am the Resurrection and the Life; he who believes in Me, though he die, yet shall he live, and whoever lives and believes in Me shall never die" (John 11: 25-26). He meant it. It's true. For you to live is Christ and to die in this life is gain (Phil. 1:21). Live your life for Christ without a care in the world. Spend and be spent even as our Lord invested His life in your well-being.

Life is the most marvelous thing in the world. How great is our God, not just for creating it but for adding that dimension to it in Jesus Christ that gives us life so abundantly that we need never fear the loss of it! Christ is risen! We *live* with Him when we are ready to *die* with Him. Have life! God has made it possible.

Text:

Truly, truly, I say to you, unless a grain of wheat falls into the earth and dies, it remains alone; but if it dies, it bears much fruit. He who loves his life loses it, and he who hates his life in this world will keep it for eternal life. (John 12: 24-25)

Lord God,
  thank You for making it possible for us to celebrate
    life in the midst of death.
  Thank You for the eternal life of Your Son
    which we accept as our guarantee
    of eternal life with You.
Encourage us to live Easter
    in the streets of our cities,
    in the places where we work and play,
    and in our dealings with all mankind.
Inspire us to live life with abandon,
    confident that we cannot lose it
    as long as we use it
    to Your glory.
We praise You for our birth
    and for our rebirth.
Accept our prayer in the name of Your risen Son. Amen.